The Pharmaceutical Guidance Navigator

A Practical Guide to Finding
Pharmaceutical Regulations, Guidelines,
and Regulatory Updates

KARIM PANJWANI

Copyright © 2024 Karim Panjwani

All rights reserved.

Copyright Notice

This work in this book is protected under copyright laws and is the sole property of Karim Panjwani, © 2024. By purchasing or using this book (inclusive of hardcopy, e-book versions, or any other format), you are agreeing to the following terms:

Primary Content

The 'Primary Content' encompasses all material in this book is subject to copyright protection. Any reproduction, transmission, downloading, or storage of the Primary Content in any information storage and retrieval system, whether electronic or mechanical, currently known or developed in the future, is strictly prohibited without the express written consent of the author of this book.

For any requests or inquiries concerning the reproduction and rights of the Primary Content, please direct your correspondence in writing to the author of this book.

The Pharmaceutical Guidance Navigator

Disclaimer

The publisher and author have applied their utmost efforts in the preparation of this book, which includes hardcopy, e-book versions, and any other formats. However, they do not provide any assurances, or guarantees regarding the accuracy or completeness of the contents of this book. They expressly disclaim any implied warranties of merchantability or suitability for a specific purpose. This book is not intended to serve as legal advice, it is provided only as a general guide. The advice, information, and templates contained within this book may not be appropriate for your situation. Some of the advice, information, or templates in this book may become outdated due to changes in industry practices, technology, or law. Neither the publisher nor the author will be held liable for any loss or other damages that may be encountered as a result of using the content of this book or acting on the advice or information contained in this book.

Trademarks

Adobe, Acrobat, FrameMaker, InDesign, and Photoshop are either registered trademarks or trademarks of Adobe Systems Incorporated in the United States and/or other countries. Apache and OpenOffice are trademarks of The Apache Software Foundation. Author-it is a registered trademark of Author-it Software Corporation. BPMN is a trademark of Object Management Group, Inc. in the United States and/or other countries. ISO is a registered trademark of the International Organization for Standardization.

Microsoft, Excel, PowerPoint, SharePoint, and Visio are either registered trademarks or trademarks of Microsoft Corporation in the United States and/or other countries. TechSmith and Snagit are registered trademarks of TechSmith Corporation. All other trademarks and registered trademarks specified in this book mentioned above or anywhere else are the property of their respective owners.

Acknowledgment

This book is the result of years of learning. I couldn't write this book without the support of my family, friends, mentors, and colleagues.

Firstly, I owe gratitude to my mentors from my educational and professional careers. Your guidance and teaching have been precious in shaping my understanding and what I am now. Without your teaching and guidance, I could not write this book.

To my peers in the industry, your companionship and shared experiences have enriched my perspective and added depth to this work. The knowledge I gained from peers, whether through formal interactions or casual conversations, has been instrumental in shaping this book.

I extend my heartfelt appreciation to all my industry colleagues who have interacted with me over the years. Your insights, experiences, and wisdom have been a constant source of inspiration. This book is a testament to our collective knowledge.

A special note of thanks to the tireless editors, researchers, and professionals who reviewed and provided valuable feedback on early drafts. Your meticulous attention to detail and constructive insights have significantly enhanced the quality of this work.

Last, but certainly not least, I am grateful to my family and friends for their unwavering support and understanding during the writing process. Your encouragement has been a source of motivation, and your belief in the importance of this endeavor has been my driving force.

In conclusion, this book is not just my creation, but a product of the collective wisdom and efforts of many. To everyone who has played a part, no matter how small, in bringing this book to fruition, I extend my deepest gratitude. Thank you.

Karim Panjwani

https://pharmacydictionary.in/
info@pharmacydictionary.in
Your Free Gift for You

As a token of my thanks for taking out time to read my book, I would like to offer you a **Free-Gift**:
Download your Free eBook PDF.

Directory of Global Health Authority Websites

List of 186 Website Links: A Comprehensive Directory of Global Health Authority Websites

To grab your **FREE GIFT,** refer to the Part 5 of this book

The Pharmaceutical Guidance Navigator

Contents

Part 1 - The Importance of Regulatory Awareness in Pharmaceuticals............... 15

Chapter 1: The Importance of Staying Current with Pharmaceutical Regulations 17

Chapter 2: How This Reference Guide Will Help Pharmaceutical Professionals 21

Part 2 - Understanding Pharmaceutical Regulatory Guidance 25

Chapter 3: Introduction to Pharmaceutical Regulatory Guidance Documents 27

Part 3 - Mastering the Art of Navigating Regulatory Websites 39

Chapter 4: Essential Skills for Extracting Information from Regulatory Websites 41

Chapter 5: United States Food and Drug Administration (FDA) Resources 43

Chapter 6: International Council for Harmonisation (ICH) Guidances........................... 77

Chapter 7: Pharmaceutical Inspection Co-operation Scheme (PIC/S) Guidance 85

Chapter 8: World Health Organization (WHO) Guidance 93

Chapter 9: Medicines and Healthcare products Regulatory Agency (MHRA) Guidance 99

Chapter 10: United States Pharmacopeia (USP) News and Updates 113

Chapter 11: European Directorate for the Quality of Medicines & Healthcare (EDQM) Guidance 117

Chapter 12: European Union (EU) Good Manufacturing Practice (GMP) Guidance 121

Chapter 13: Therapeutic Goods Administration (TGA) Guidance (Australia) 137

Chapter 14: Health Canada Guidance 151

Chapter 15: Pharmaceuticals and Medical Devices Agency (PMDA), Japan Guidance 159

Chapter 16: Agência Nacional de Vigilância Sanitária (ANVISA) - Brazilian Regulations 167

Chapter 17: South African Health Products Regulatory Authority (SAHPRA) Regulations 171

Chapter 18: Active Pharmaceutical Ingredients Committee (APIC) Guidance 175

Part 4 - Staying Informed: Resources for Ongoing Updates 179

Chapter 19: Regulatory Affairs Professionals Society (RAPS) for Regulatory News Updates 181

Part 5 - Free Gift 185

About the Author 189

The Pharmaceutical Guidance Navigator

Part 1 - The Importance of Regulatory Awareness in Pharmaceuticals

The Pharmaceutical Guidance Navigator

Chapter 1: The Importance of Staying Current with Pharmaceutical Regulations

As pharmaceutical professionals, navigating the intricate web of regulations and guidance is paramount to our success. From research and development to manufacturing and marketing, staying abreast of constant changes is not just optional – it's an essential safeguard for individual careers and the industry's well-being.

A. Here's why staying updated is critical:

1. Compliance & Risk Management:

Non-compliance with regulations can lead to regulatory non-compliance, reputational damage, and loss of business in the respective markets. By staying informed, you proactively mitigate risks, ensuring current Good Manufacturing Practice and regulatory expectations are met for requirements specified by intended market regulatory guidance.

2. Informed Decision-Making:

Regulatory updates often unveil improvement opportunities and help you proactively act on the upcoming regulatory expectations. Understanding these changes empowers you to make informed decisions about development strategies, resource allocation, and understand potential implications when there is a possibility of delay in implementation of requirements.

3. Competitive Advantage:

Keeping pace with advancements allows you to be ahead in the competition and will attract more business since you would be the among the first who have implemented the regulatory requirements and give your organization a change to set a benchmark. This agility grants you a competitive edge, positioning you to capitalize on new markets and technologies.

4. Building Trust and Credibility:

Demonstrating expertise in regulatory compliance fosters trust with patients, authorities, and colleagues. Regularly updating your knowledge showcases your commitment to ethical practices and patient safety.

B. Benefits for Freshers and Young Professionals:

For those new to the field, staying updated is even more crucial.

1. Solid Foundation:

A grounded understanding of current regulations forms the foundation for your professional growth.

2 Navigating Complexity:

The pharma landscape is ever-changing, and early exposure equips you with the skills to adapt and thrive in this dynamic environment.

3. Networking Opportunities:

By actively engaging with regulatory updates, you demonstrate initiative and spark conversations with experienced professionals, fostering valuable networking opportunities.

4. Growth Opportunities:

When you are looking for new opportunities in your dream organization, your updated knowledge will help you stand out among the candidates and the probability of getting opportunity would be much higher compared to others who are not updated with current knowledge.

C. The Power of Updated Guidance in Inspections and Citations:

When you are subject to inspections or potential citations, possessing a thorough understanding of the latest guidelines can be lifesaver for you in following ways:

1. Demonstrating Compliance:

Presenting evidence of adhering to the latest regulations shows good faith and minimizes the risk of non-compliance and builds trust in your organization indicating that you are willing to keep your system updated all the time.

2. Proactive Mitigation:

By illustrating the impact of new guidelines on your strategies, you can showcase your forward-thinking approach to compliance and risk reduction. This will enable you to strategically distribute resources and budget your requirements well before the effective date of guidance implementation requirements.

3. Building Rapport:

Showcasing your knowledge of recent changes fosters a more collaborative and productive interaction with inspectors, potentially leading to favorable outcomes.

Chapter 2: How This Reference Guide Will Help Pharmaceutical Professionals

The complex and ever-evolving nature of the pharmaceutical industry makes staying abreast of regulatory updates an essential yet overwhelming task for professionals. Navigating the vast amount of information scattered across websites and documents demands significant time and effort.

A. Challenges faced by professionals:

Information overload:

Countless regulatory bodies and organizations (e.g., FDA, EMA, WHO) regularly publish updates, and to keep track and navigation the current guidelines and update is difficult task and searching guidance randomly on the internet may end up you picking older versions of guidance or old update.

Difficulty in finding relevant information:

All the regulatory body websites are designed differently, sometimes, there is no search function available and files are just located on some pages as pdf files. And sometimes, it is difficult to locate the right pages even if you Google it. When searching for any specific guideline on Google, there is a possibility that google will give the result of the old version of guideline because of various Google algorithms and you end up using the old version of guidance.

Lack of consolidated resources:

Absence of a central repository or consolidated document available forces professionals to visit multiple sites, increasing time and frustration.

Resource Tracking Challenges:

Hard to remember or track relevant resources when it is needed and end up with frustrating experience or seeking consultation from experts.

Inconsistent referencing and interpretation:

Sometimes, it happens that when you are referring to the guidelines, two people in the same organization find two different documents and it is hard to figure out which one to refer to as the correct reference for the right purpose.

B. Benefits of a Ready Reference Guide:

Organized search guide:

Streamlines access to current regulatory guidance from various sources.

Clear organization:

Facilitates finding specific information quickly and easily.

Regular updates:

Keeps professionals informed of the latest changes proactively.

Improved compliance:

Reduces risks by ensuring awareness of all relevant regulations.

Increased efficiency:

Saves time and effort. Equips professionals with the latest and accurate knowledge for better decision-making.

C. Conclusion:

In a dynamic and demanding industry, access to reliable and readily available guidance is crucial for pharmaceutical professionals. This guide is created for pharmaceutical professionals as a Ready Reference Guide that will be a valuable tool, empowering them to navigate right regulations efficiently, ensuring compliance, and achieving success and keep you ahead of the industry and other organizations.

To fulfill this requirement of industry professionals, I have created this booklet as a guide to navigating different regulatory websites effectively.

Part 2 - Understanding Pharmaceutical Regulatory Guidance

The Pharmaceutical Guidance Navigator

Chapter 3: Introduction to Pharmaceutical Regulatory Guidance Documents

The pharmaceutical industry operates within a complex web of regional and global regulations, ensuring the safety, efficacy, and quality of medicines reaching patients worldwide.

Firstly, let's understand what types of guidance and reference documents are available for the pharmaceutical professionals. Secondly, we need to identify what are the must-to-follow documents in this field. Thirdly, it's important to know what are the guidance documents that are not mandatory to follow. Despite not being mandatory, regulators still expect the industry to use these documents. The reason behind this expectation is to improve the overall quality systems, product quality, and patient safety. The requirements are mainly categorized in the following three categories:

- **Regional Regulatory Bodies:** The

Gatekeepers

- **Global Organizations:** Setting the Standards

- **Industry Associations and Resources:** Support and Advocacy

1. Regional Regulatory Bodies:

Regional Regulatory Bodies are the Direct Authority. These institutions hold the official power to approve or reject manufacturing, storage or distribution of drugs within their specific jurisdiction and to the applications who have applied in respective regions for the purpose of marketing and supply. The key functions of Regional Regulatory Bodies are:

- These are the gatekeepers for specific geographic areas.

- They set standards for drug safety, efficacy, and quality, and grant approval for medications sold within their jurisdiction.

- Set and enforce regulations for drug development, approval, and marketing.

- Conduct inspections of manufacturing facilities.

- Provide guidance documents and resources for industry stakeholders.

- Each body has unique requirements and procedures, making navigating them crucial for specific market entry.

Examples of regulatory bodies are as follows:

A. US Food and Drug Administration (FDA):

The primary regulatory body for the US market, providing extensive guidance documents, regulations, and resources for drug development, approval, and marketing.

https://www.fda.gov/

B. European Medicines Agency (EMA) and National Competent Authorities (NCAs):

The EMA oversees centralized approval for the European Union, with NCAs handling national-specific matters. Explore EMA guidelines and NCA websites for regional nuances.

https://www.ema.europa.eu/

C. Japan Pharmaceuticals and Medical Devices Agency (PMDA):

Responsible for drug regulation in Japan, offering Japanese translations of relevant guidelines and specific requirements.

https://www.pmda.go.jp/english/

D. Health Canada:

Oversees drug regulation in Canada, providing guidance specific to the Canadian market.

https://www.canada.ca/en/health-canada.html

E. Therapeutic Goods Administration (TGA) Australia:

Regulates medicines and medical devices in Australia, offering dedicated resources for understanding its processes.

https://www.tga.gov.au/

F. Medicines and Healthcare products Regulatory Agency (MHRA) UK:

Ensures the safety and quality of medicines in the UK, providing guidance and regulations specific to its jurisdiction.
https://www.gov.uk/government/organisations/medicines-and-healthcare-products-regulatory-agency

G. China National Medical Products Administration (NMPA):

Regulates drugs in China, with translated guidance and specific requirements to navigate.

https://english.nmpa.gov.cn/

H. Brazil Health Surveillance Agency (ANVISA): Oversees drug regulation in Brazil, offering resources in Portuguese.

https://www.gov.br/anvisa/

2. Global Organizations:

They don't directly approve manufacturing facilities and drug products, but their efforts influence regional bodies and set international standards. They promote harmonization, consistency, and best practices across different regions. They develop global standards, guidelines, and best practices for drug development and regulation. Key functions of Global Organizations are:

- Develop international standards and guidelines for drug development and registration.

- Share best practices and information between regulatory authorities.

- Facilitate global access to safe and effective medicines.

- These entities focus on harmonizing regulations across different regions.

- They streamline processes and promote consistency in drug evaluation across borders.

Examples of Global Organizations are as follows:

A. World Health Organization (WHO):

Sets international standards for drugs and provides pre-qualification programs for global access. WHO conducts inspections of manufacturing facilities for medicines that are procured by UN agencies. These inspections are not for the purpose of approving the facility, but rather to assess compliance with WHO GMP standards and identify any areas for improvement. The findings of the inspection are shared with the national regulatory authority of the country where the facility is located.

https://www.who.int/teams/health-product-policy-and-standards/standards-and-specifications/norms-and-standards-for-pharmaceuticals

B. International Council for Harmonization (ICH):

Develops harmonized guidelines aiming for global consistency.

https://www.ich.org/

C. Pharmaceutical Inspection Co-operation Scheme (PIC/S):

Promotes harmonized GMP (Good Manufacturing Practice) inspection and regulatory practices.

https://picscheme.org/

D. European Directorate for the Quality of Medicines (EDQM):

Sets standards for the quality of medicines in Europe, with resources relevant to global manufacturers.
https://www.edqm.eu/en/

3. Industry Associations and Resources:

Industry Associations and Resources don't regulate drugs but provide valuable information, advocacy, and resources to the industry. They offer industry insights, support compliance, and advocate for industry needs. Provide information, resources, and advocacy for the pharmaceutical industry. Key functions of Industry Associations and Resources are:

- Offer educational programs and training for industry professionals.

- Provide industry-specific information and resources.

- Advocate for policies that support innovation and access to medicines.

- These groups offer support and information to pharmaceutical professionals.

- They provide guidance on regulations, advocacy for the industry, and educational resources.

Examples of Industry Associations and Resources are as follows:

A. American Association of Pharmaceutical Scientists (AAPS):

AAPS is a non-profit scientific organization with a global reach, focusing on advancing the pharmaceutical sciences through scientific meetings, publications, and professional development programs. They offer various resources for members, including access to scientific publications, networking opportunities, and continuing education courses. Their services are primarily paid in nature through membership fees, although they may offer some free resources or events.

https://www.aaps.org/

B. European Federation of Pharmaceutical Industries and Associations (EFPIA):

EFPIA represents the research-based pharmaceutical industry in Europe. They advocate for policies that support innovation and access to medicines, and they provide a platform for collaboration among member companies. EFPIA's services are primarily paid through membership fees, although they may offer some free publications or events.

https://www.efpia.eu/

C. Parenteral Drug Association (PDA):

PDA is a global non-profit organization focused on the science and technology of parenteral drug products, which are those administered through injection. They offer resources and education for professionals involved in the development, manufacturing, and quality control of these products. PDA offers a mix of free and paid services, including publications, webinars, and conferences.

https://www.pda.org/

D. International Federation of Pharmaceutical Manufacturers and Associations (IFPMA):

IFPMA represents the global pharmaceutical industry. They advocate for policies that support innovation and access to medicines, and they provide a platform for collaboration among member companies. IFPMA's services are primarily paid through membership fees, although they may offer some free publications or events.

https://www.ifpma.org/

E. International Society for Pharmaceutical Engineering (ISPE):

ISPE is a non-profit organization that provides resources and education for professionals involved in the design, construction, operation, and maintenance of pharmaceutical manufacturing facilities. They offer training courses, publications, and networking opportunities for members. ISPE offers a mix of free and paid services, including publications, webinars, certification programs, and conferences.

https://ispe.org/

F. PhRMA (Pharmaceutical Research and Manufacturers of America):

PhRMA is the leading trade association representing the research-based pharmaceutical industry in the United States. They advocate for policies that support innovation and access to medicines, and they provide a platform for collaboration among member companies. PhRMA's services are primarily paid through membership fees, although they may offer some free publications or events.

https://phrma.org/en

G. American Society for Testing and Materials (ASTM International):

ASTM International is a global standards development organization that provides a wide range of technical standards for various industries, including the pharmaceutical industry. These standards help ensure the quality and safety of pharmaceutical products. ASTM offers a mix of free and paid services, including access to standards, training courses, and proficiency testing programs.

https://www.astm.org/

H. Indian Pharmaceutical Alliance (IPA):

IPA is the apex national organization representing the Indian pharmaceutical industry. They advocate for policies that support the growth of the industry, and they provide a platform for collaboration among member companies. IPA offers a mix of free and paid services to its members, including access to information, training programs, and networking opportunities.

https://www.ipa-india.org/

The Pharmaceutical Guidance Navigator

Part 3 - Mastering the Art of Navigating Regulatory Websites

The Pharmaceutical Guidance Navigator

Chapter 4: Essential Skills for Extracting Information from Regulatory Websites

In the previous chapter, we delved into the details of different organizations and their roles and influence on the pharmaceutical industry. We discovered the pivotal roles of Regional Regulatory Bodies as gatekeepers, the influence of Global Organizations in standard-setting, and the support provided by Industry Associations and Resources in fostering innovation and collaboration.

As we turn the page to this new chapter, we will embark on a detailed exploration of the websites of these key Regional Regulatory Bodies and Global Organizations. Our journey will guide us through the maze of their online resources, teaching us how to effectively navigate these sites to unearth essential information. We will learn where to locate crucial guidance, stay abreast of the latest updates, and learn to search how to find the regulatory and accreditation status of various pharmaceuticals. Let's get started.

Chapter 5: United States Food and Drug Administration (FDA) Resources

The US Food and Drug Administration (FDA) website is a vast library of information, but it can be tricky to navigate. This guide will simplify your search and help you find the specific guidance documents you need.

The FDA website offers more than just guidance documents. You can also find information on:

- Recently added guidance documents

- The FDA's rules and regulations and any recent updates

- Warning letters the FDA sends to companies

- Site classifications assigned to pharmaceutical manufacturing facilities

While this guide focuses on mastering the guidance

documents section, don't worry! I will show you how to find them quickly, either by browsing directly or using powerful search tools. Whether you prefer a simple search using keywords or want to narrow down your results with specific details, this guide will turn you into an FDA website pro in no time!

A. Search for FDA Guidance Documents:

1. **Access the Page:** Open your preferred web browser and navigate to the 'FDA Guidance Documents' page using the link https://www.fda.gov/regulatory-information/search-fda-guidance-documents

   Or Scan QR Code

   This is the starting point for accessing all FDA guidance documents.

   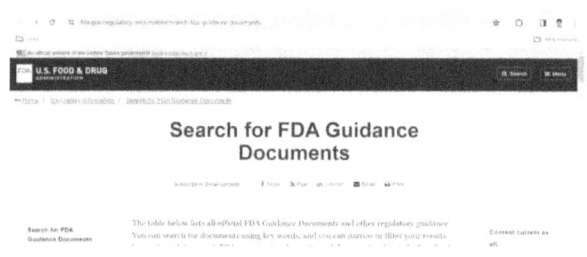

You can directly navigate the guidelines by using the dropdown menus as shown in the following image or search the documents using the Keyword Search tool explained in the next point.

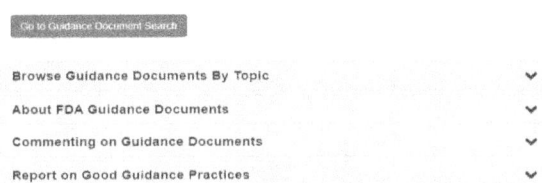

2. **Keyword Search:** The search bar provided in the page is your primary tool for finding specific documents. Enter keywords related to the guidance document you're looking for. For instance, if you're interested in "drug labeling", type these words into the search bar. The search tool will filter and return all guidance documents that contain entered keywords. See the following example with a screenshot. The search tool gave results as follows with the output "Showing 1 to 10 of 159 entries (filtered from 2,721 total entries)"

Guidance Document Search

Search: drug labeling

Showing 1 to 10 of 159 entries (filtered from 2,721 total entries)

Filters

Product	FDA Organization
Topic	Issue Date
Draft or Final	Open for Comment
Document Type	Comment Closing Date on Draft

Export Excel

ummary	Document	Issue Date	FDA Organization	Topic	Guidance Status
Revising ANDA Labeling Following Revision of the	PDF (260.85 KB)	01/24/2024	Center for Drug Evaluation and	Generic Drugs	Final

3. **Use Filters:** You can use filters located below the search bar to refine your search results further to get specific guidance documents. Here's a more detailed look at each filter:

    Product: Select the type of product (e.g., drug, device, food, tobacco) that the guidance document pertains to.

    Date Issued: If you're looking for documents issued within a specific timeframe, use this filter. You can choose a custom date range or one of the preset options.

    FDA Organizational Unit: This filter lets you select documents issued by a specific FDA organizational unit. For example, if you're only interested in documents issued by the Center for Drug Evaluation and Research, select this option from the dropdown menu.

Type of Document: Use this filter to select the type of document you're looking for. Options include guidance, rule, proposed rule, final rule, etc.

Draft or Final Status: Use this filter to select whether you want to view draft documents, final documents, or both.

Comment Period: If you're interested in documents that are currently open for comment, use this filter.

4. **Browse by Topic:** Underneath the search filter tool, it provides a list of all the guidelines. If you're not sure what to search for, or if you're having trouble finding a specific document, you can browse separate collections of guidance documents by topic. This can be a great way to discover relevant documents that you might not have found through a keyword search.

5. **Commenting on Guidance Documents:** The FDA values input from the public on its guidance documents. If you're interested in providing feedback on a document, look for opportunities to provide input into guidance development. You can see the last column "Open for Comment" and identify which

guidance document is open for the comment and you can review and provide comments on the guideline as per timeline provided by FDA.

In this way you can navigate the required guidance document that is published by the U.S. FDA. It is very essential to understand the nature of guidelines. In the initial pages of the guidelines, it explains that whether the guidance is with remark "Contains Nonbinding Recommendations" or it is preferred guidance. Sometimes FDA provides declarations as follows;

"This guidance represents the Food and Drug Administration's (FDA's) current thinking on this topic. It does not create or confer any rights for or on any person and does not operate to bind FDA or the public. You can use an alternative approach if the approach satisfies the requirements of the applicable statutes and regulations. If you want to discuss an alternative approach, contact the FDA staff responsible for implementing this guidance. If you cannot identify the appropriate FDA staff, call the appropriate number listed on the title page of this guidance. "

Even though FDA gives these declarations, the guidelines are created by FDA experts and comments from industry, it is worth using and implementing the guidelines. Most pharma professionals expect that these are the industry standards to refer to and follow it by the organizations.

B. Newly Added FDA Guidance Documents:

This section of the US FDA site helps you navigate the newly added guideline published by the US FDA. Let's see how to navigate this page.

1. **Opening the Page:**

   - Open your web browser.

   - Type in the URL:

     https://www.fda.gov/drugs/guidances-drugs/newly-added-guidance-documents or simply click on the link or Scan QR Code.

2. **Understanding the Page Layout:**

   - The page you see is a list of documents. Each row in the list is a different document.

   - Each document has a Topic, Guidance Status, and Date. The Topic tells you what the document is about. The Guidance Status tells you if the document is a draft or a final version. The Date tells you when the document was added to the website.

3. Searching for Specific Documents:

- If you're looking for a specific document, you can use the search function.

- For example, I have provided the keyword "Validation", it shows all the newly published guidance having requested the keyword. Refer to the following screenshot.

- This is the excellent way to locate the newly published guidance document by FDA.

4. Sorting the Documents:

You can change the order of the documents in the list. To do this, click on the column headers: Topic, Guidance, Status (Draft or Final), or Date. Clicking on a column header will sort the documents based on that column.

5. Reading the Guidance Document:

Once you've found a document you're interested in, click on guidance title. This will navigate to you to the full text of the document for you to read or PDF document to open and download.

C. Referring the Code of Federal Regulation (CFR) and Searching for Current Regulations and Changes:

Code of Federal Regulation or CFR is a mandatory requirement as it is the regulation. 21 CFR, or Title 21 of the Code of Federal Regulations, is a database of rules for the Food and Drug Administration (FDA). When any company or organization wants to provide healthcare services or supply products to US territory, 21 CFR is applicable and mandatory to follow. No deviation to the provided regulation is acceptable and any deviation to the regulation would result in the regulatory citation for noncompliance.

Let's understand how to access the 21 CFR and how to check for the updates in the regulation.

Access the Website: Open your web browser and type in the URL or Scan QR Code:

https://www.accessdata.fda.gov/scripts/cdrh/cfdocs/cfcfr/cfrsearch.cfm

The Pharmaceutical Guidance Navigator

it will navigate to the following page.

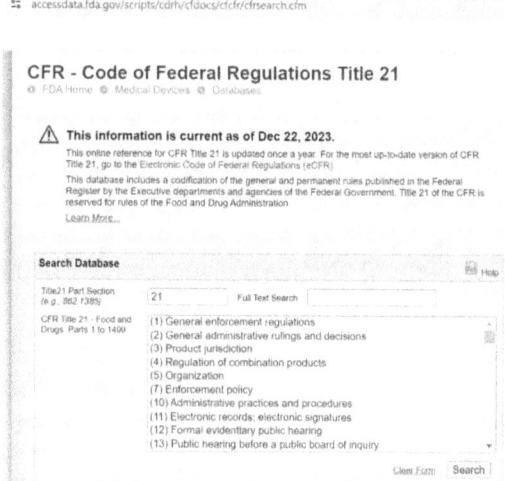

You can search any applicable chapter by writing the part number or full text in the search bar as shown in the above screenshot.

If you read the warning provided at the top of the page, it says that "This information is current as of Dec 22, 2023, this online reference for CFR Title 21 is updated once a year. For the most up-to-date version of CFR Title 21, go to the Electronic Code of Federal Regulations (eCFR)."

The link has the URL https://www.ecfr.gov/ or Scan QR Code.

The above warning indicates that if you want to refer to the most updated version of CFR, you need to use the following URL.

1. **Navigate to the URL**:

   https://www.ecfr.gov/ or simply click on the link.

2. **Homepage Overview:**

   The homepage displays a list of Titles, each representing a broad area subject to federal regulation. Each Title has a 'Last Amended' date and a 'view changes' link if there have been recent changes. This feature is very useful on this page as you can refer to the changes done during the last update. Refer to the following screenshot.

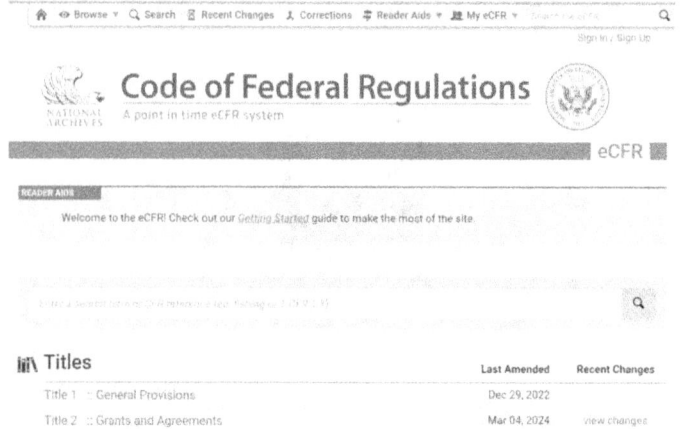

3. Navigating to the Content of Interest:

You can navigate to a specific Title by clicking on it from the homepage. This will take you to a page with a list of Parts under that Title.

4. Browsing and Searching:

You can browse through the Parts or use the search function to find specific terms. The search function is located at the top right of the page.

5. Reading eCFR Content:

Click on a Part to view its content. The content is organized into Sections. Each Section is further divided into paragraphs for easy reading.

6. eCFR Changes Through Time:

You can view a timeline of how the CFR content has changed over time. This feature allows you to review the latest changes as well as previous changes. Also, you can verify the changes done after the specific date by selecting the specific date. Refer to the following screenshot.

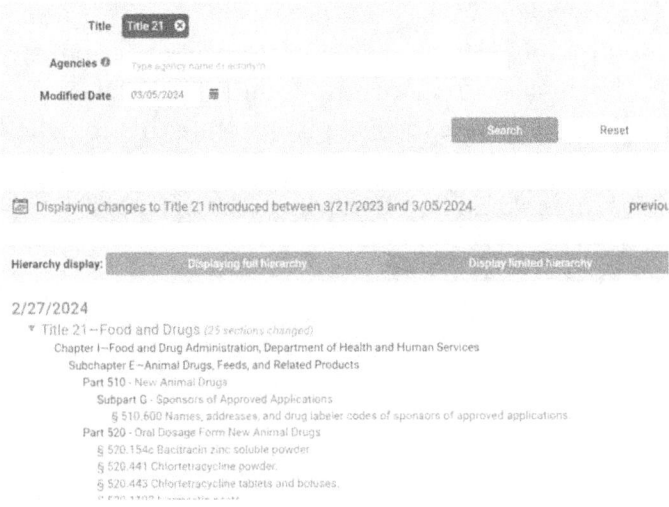

Using the above process, you can refer to the current regulations and recent changes and keep yourself updated.

D. Understanding Warning Letters:

During inspection, when FDA finds that a manufacturer has significantly violated FDA regulations, they notify the manufacturer. This notification is often in the form of a Warning Letter.

The examples of violations are poor manufacturing practices, problems with claims for what a product can do, or incorrect directions for use.

The purpose of the letter is to give a clear message to the company that they must correct the problem and provide directions and a timeframe within which the company needs to correct the situation.

The provided database of the warning letters is a very useful tool for the pharmaceutical industry professionals to learn from others' mistakes and proactively ensure the compliance status of their sites.

Let's understand how to navigate the web page.

1. **Opening the Page:**

   - Open your web browser.

   - Type in the URL:

     https://www.fda.gov/inspections-compliance-enforcement-and-criminal-investigations/compliance-actions-and-activities/warning-letters or simply click on the link or Scan QR Code.

It will open the following page.

Warning Letters

Subscribe to Email Updates   f Share   X Post   in LinkedIn   ✉ Email   🖨 Print

Learn about the types of warning letters on FDA's website.

- Matters described in FDA warning letters may have been subject to subsequent interaction between FDA and the letter recipient that may have changed the regulatory status of issues discussed in the letter.
- To obtain additional available information, contact FDA. Requests to FDA for agency records should be sent to: Food and Drug Administration Division of Freedom of Information (HFI-35), 5630 Fishers Lane, Rockville, MD 20857. Instructions for how to submit an FOI request can be found at How to Make a FOIA Request.

Search

Filter by

Issuing Office

Letter Issue Date   Letters with Response or Closeout

2. Understanding the Page Layout and Searching for Specific Warning Letters:

- At the page, you'll see a search bar.

- Enter keywords related to the warning letter you're looking for, such as the company name or the Issuing Office.

- The list of applicable warning letters will be displayed on the page.

3. Filtering the Search Results:

- Furthermore, you can refine your results using the filters.

- You can filter by Posted Date, Letter Issue Date, Issuing Office, and Year.

- On applying the filters, you can find the relevant warning letters.

4. Understanding the table:

- The page you see is a list of warning letters. Each row in the list is a different warning letter.

- Each warning letter has a Posted Date, Letter Issue Date, Company Name, Issuing Office, Subject, and Response Letter. The Posted Date tells you when the warning letter was posted on the website. The Letter Issue Date tells you when the warning letter was issued. The Company Name tells you the name of the company that received the warning letter. The Issuing Office tells you which FDA office issued the warning letter. The Subject tells you what the warning letter is about. The Response Letter links to the company's response to the warning letter and the closeout letter, if available.

5. **Navigating the List:**

   You can scroll through the list to view the warning letters. The list is organized by the Posted Date, with the most recent warning letters at the top.

6. **Reading a Warning Letter:**

   To read a warning letter, click on the link in the row of the warning letter you are interested in. This will take you to a page with the full text of the warning letter.

E. Unveiling a Pharmaceutical Company's Site Classification with the FDA

After conducting an inspection, the Food and Drug Administration (FDA) evaluates whether the areas examined comply with relevant laws and regulations. Based on the investigation, FDA assigns one of three classifications to the inspection. Meaning of each classification is explained below:

No Action Indicated (NAI):

This classification indicates that no objectionable conditions or practices were found during the inspection, or if any objectionable conditions were identified, they do not warrant further regulatory action.

Voluntary Action Indicated (VAI):

When this classification is assigned, it means that objectionable conditions or practices were observed, but the agency is not currently prepared to recommend any administrative or regulatory action.

Official Action Indicated (OAI):

This classification signifies that regulatory and/or administrative actions will be recommended as a result of the inspection.

Knowing a company's inspection classification is crucial, especially when you are receiving any service or material from other organizations. This could involve procuring Active Pharmaceutical Ingredients (APIs), or getting your product or material tested from a laboratory that caters to the US market. Another scenario could be if you are a contract giver intending to get a product manufactured from another organization for supply to the US. In such cases, it becomes important to understand the respective site classification by the U. S. FDA to assess the risk involved. This understanding becomes particularly important when you are exploring the above services. By understanding the site compliance history and trend, you can make an informed decision about whether or not to choose that firm.

Let's explore the web pages to the FDA dashboard to understand the site classification and inspection history.

The Pharmaceutical Guidance Navigator

1. **Opening the Page:**

- Open your web browser.

- Type in the URL:

  https://www.fda.gov/inspections-compliance-enforcement-and-criminal-investigations/inspection-classification-database or simply click on the link or scan QR Code.

It will open the following page.

Inspection Classification Database

f Share   X Post   in LinkedIn   ✉ Email   🖨 Print

Important Notes:

- Not all inspections are included in the database. Inspections conducted by States, pre-approval inspections, mammography facility inspections, inspections waiting for a final enforcement action, and inspections of nonclinical labs are not included. Inspections of nonclinical labs are available at Nonclinical Laboratories Inspected under Good Laboratory Practices.

- The results show final classifications of No Action Indicated (NAI), Voluntary Action Indicated (VAI), Official Action Indicated (OAI) for each project area within an inspection.

The Food and Drug Administration (FDA) conducts inspections and assessments of regulated facilities to determine a firm's compliance with applicable laws and regulations, such as the Food, Drug, and Cosmetic Act and related Acts.

FDA discloses a segment of inspection information to help improve the public's understanding of how the FDA works to protect the public health. Disclosure of a firm's inspection information encourages firm compliance and provides the public with an understanding of the Agency's enforcement actions and an ability to make more informed marketplace choices.

Inspection Classification Database and Search

- Please use the FDA Data Dashboard for Inspection Classification data. The Inspection Classification Database dataset and search functionality have been decommissioned.

2. Steps to Navigate the inspection classification dashboard:

After opening the above page, https://www.fda.gov/inspections-compliance-enforcement-and-criminal-investigations/inspection-classification-database, clicks on the "FDA Data Dashboard" link (https://datadashboard.fda.gov/ora/cd/inspections.htm).

It will open the following page. The page has different dashboards that provide you details of Foreign (Other than US) and Domestic (US) inspection details, Inspection classification, Top 10 citations, Table containing Inspections Details with site classification, and Inspections Citations Details table with applicable CFR clause and description of citation.

The Pharmaceutical Guidance Navigator

The Pharmaceutical Guidance Navigator

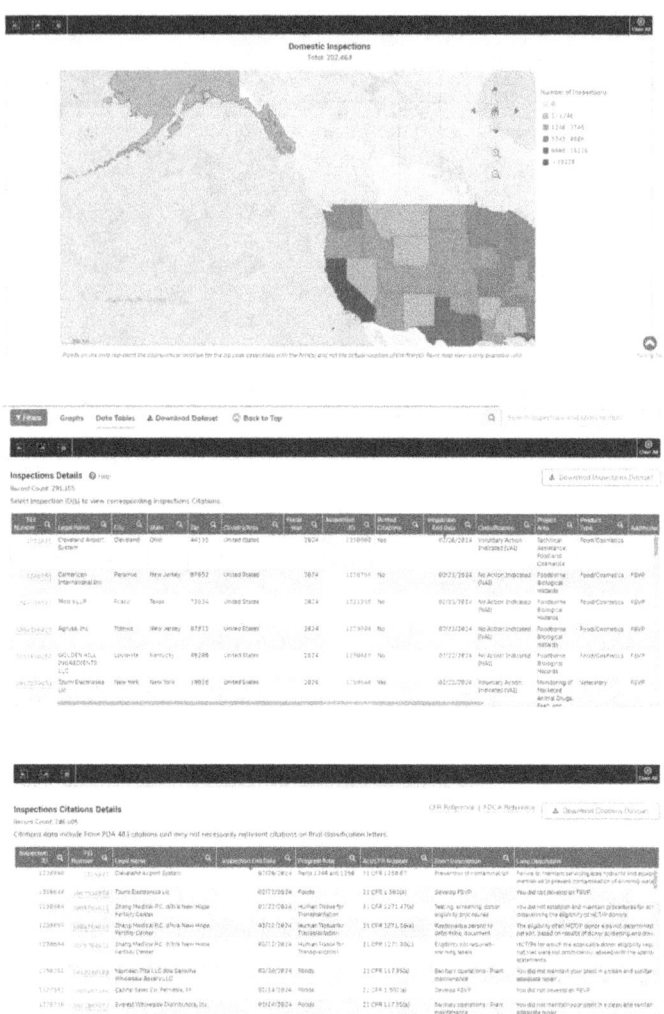

On the top right of the page, you can find the search bar, where you can enter specific details such as company name, country name, state name and you can narrow down the search and get specific details. Refer to the following screenshot as an example.

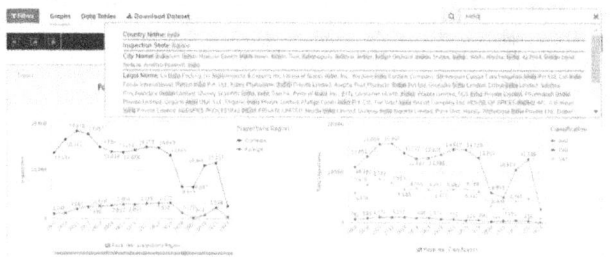

After this macro search, you can do further microlevel search using the tables, such as company name, classification, and any other fields available in the table header. Refer to the following example.

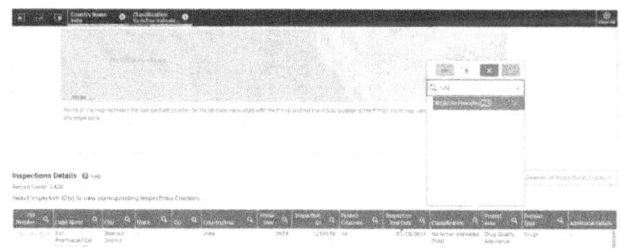

There is one more top-level filter available on the top left of the page using which you can apply multiple filters at once. Refer to the following example where Fiscal Year and Country Name is applied as a filter and it provides specific information as follows.

The site also allows you to Download the dataset in the spreadsheet format.

F. Exploring the Compliance Dashboards on U.S. FDA website:

The webpage of the Compliance Dashboards by U.S. FDA allows users to explore and analyze public FDA data within various compliance-related datasets. Here's a summary of its key features and how it can be helpful:

- **Inspections:** This section provides data on U.S. domestic and foreign inspections by fiscal year, classification, product type, etc. It helps users understand the compliance status of regulated facilities.

- **Compliance Actions:** This includes data on warning letters, injunctions, and seizures by fiscal year, product type, etc. It provides insights into the actions taken by the FDA to enforce compliance.

- **Recalls:** This section provides data on recalls by fiscal year, classification, product type, status, etc.

It helps users stay informed about product safety issues.

- **Imports and refusals:** This includes summary data, refusals, and entry data by various parameters like fiscal year, product categories, countries, etc.

The data used in these dashboards is sourced from FDA compliance and enforcement data that is cleared for public access. The dashboard is continuously updated with additional sources. Each dashboard page includes guidance on the data used, any limitations, and clarifications regarding what the data represents.

This Compliance Dashboard is a valuable resource for anyone interested in FDA compliance and enforcement activities. It provides a comprehensive view of the FDA's efforts to ensure the safety and efficacy of regulated products. Whether you're a researcher, a regulated firm, consumer, or a consultant, this dashboard can provide useful insights into the FDA's regulatory activities.

Let's understand how to navigate the web page.

1. **Opening the Page:**

   - Open your web browser. Type in the URL: https://datadashboard.fda.gov/ora/cd/index.htm or simply click on the link or scan QR code.

The Pharmaceutical Guidance Navigator

It will open the following page.

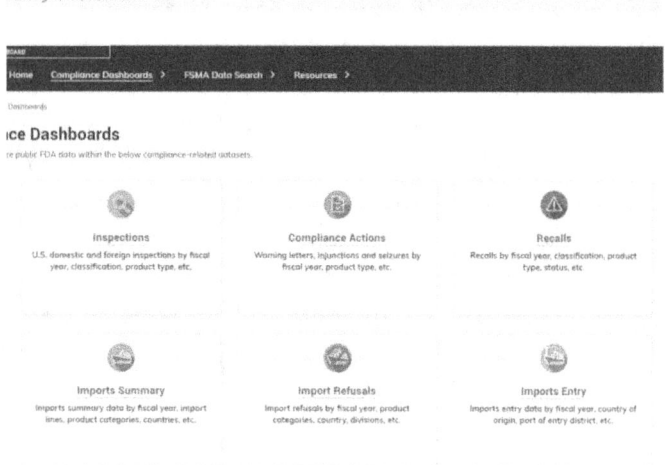

2. Understanding the Page Layout:

- On the page, to navigate to each of the items, you can click on the respective links and explore the respective pages. We already have discussed one of the above dashboards, which is the Inspections dashboard.

- You can explore each dashboard in a similar manner as I have explained about the Inspection Dashboard in the previous section.

G. Exploring ORA FOIA Electronic Reading Room:

ORA FOIA Electronic Reading Room provided by the U.S. Food and Drug Administration (FDA). This page (https://www.fda.gov/about-fda/office-regulatory-affairs/ora-foia-electronic-reading-room)

is a valuable resource for pharmaceutical professionals for several reasons:

Inspection Records: The ORA Electronic Reading Room displays copies of ORA domestic (US) inspection and related records. These records can provide insights into the FDA's inspection process and findings, which can help pharmaceutical professionals understand the regulatory expectations and improve their own compliance.

Publicly Available Data: The page makes these records publicly available either proactively at their discretion or because they are frequently requested. This transparency can help professionals stay informed about the latest developments and trends in the industry.

FOIA Requests: If professionals are unable to find documents that they are looking for, they may file a

FOIA (Freedom of Information Act) request for the records. This allows professionals to access specific information that may not be readily available.

Archived Content: Content for the ORA FOIA Electronic Reading Room is available on FDA's website for five years before being archived. This provides a historical perspective on regulatory affairs, which can be useful for trend analysis and strategic planning.

Specific Records: The page provides specific records are as follows;

- 483

- 483 Response

- Adverse Determination Letter

- Adverse Determination Letter Response

- Amended 483

- Consent Decree

- Consent Decree Correspondence

- Consumer Complaint Record

- Establishment Inspection Report (EIR)

- Exhibits and Attachments

- FDA Requested Recall Letter
- FMD-145 Letter
- Investigation Memo
- Memo
- Other Correspondence
- Recall Record
- Receipt of Payment Letter
- Response
- Resumption of Operations Authorization Letter
- Sample Record
- State Referral Letter
- Untitled Letter
- Warning Letter Response
- Workplan

Let's understand how to navigate the web page.

1. Opening the Page:

- Open your web browser.

- Type in the URL: https://www.fda.gov/about-fda/office-regulatory-affairs/ora-foia-electronic-reading-room or simply click on the link or Scan QR Code.

It will open the following page.

2. Understanding the Page Layout:

- To identify the specific record that you are looking for, you can use the search bar and write the keyword that you are looking for and then you can further narrow down the search using the filter option underneath the search bar.

- As you find the document, you can click on the link in the table, under the heading "Record Type" and it will open the selected document.

- When I was going through this page, I found an interesting type of document called "483 Response" and "Warning Letter Response". These documents are useful for the industry to refer to, learn from, and identify differences in how other organizations are responding to identified non-compliances. Best practices can be adopted from these. However, a word of caution is necessary here. We do not know whether the FDA accepted the response or not, or whether organizations sent other follow-up responses to the FDA. Therefore, we cannot consider these responses as a standard for similar observations. The response given by the respective company is unique to their situation and is not a standard declared by the agency.

H. Exploring 483s and Compliance Records on US FDA site:

In this section, I am discussing the page, "Frequently Requested or Proactively Posted Compliance Records" section of the FDA's website (https://www.fda.gov/drugs/cder-foia-electronic-reading-room/frequently-requested-or-proactively-posted-compliance-records).

This page is a part of the Center for Drug Evaluation and Research (CDER) Freedom of Information Act (FOIA) Electronic Reading Room. The page provides access to frequently requested or proactively posted compliance records related to various pharmaceutical firms, such as Untitled Letter, Import Alert Notification Letter, EIR, and 483s.

Let's understand how to navigate the web page.

1. Opening the Page:

- Open your web browser.

- Type in the URL:

    https://www.fda.gov/drugs/cder-foia-electronic-reading-room/frequently-requested-or-proactively-posted-compliance-records or simply click on the link or scan QR Code.

It will open the following page.

Frequently Requested or Proactively Posted Compliance Records

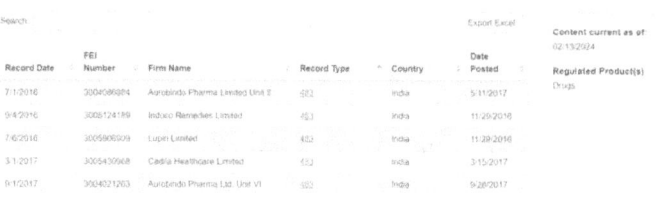

2. **Understanding the Page Layout:**

To refer to the specific document, such as 483, click on the link under the heading "Record Type". On clicking the link, it will open the required record and you can refer to it or you can download the record for your future reference.

3. **Here's how it can be beneficial for pharmaceutical professionals:**

Access to Compliance Records: The page provides access to frequently requested or proactively posted compliance records related to various pharmaceutical firms. These records include inspection reports, 483s, warning letters, and other compliance-related documents from firms worldwide.

Insight into Regulatory Standards: By studying these records, you can gain insights into the FDA's regulatory standards and expectations. You can understand common areas of non-compliance and take proactive measures to ensure their practices meet FDA guidelines.

Benchmarking and Learning: The records can serve as a benchmark for pharmaceutical companies to compare their own practices and processes. They can learn from the mistakes and best practices of other companies.

Chapter 6: International Council for Harmonisation (ICH) Guidance

The International Council for Harmonisation of Technical Requirements for Pharmaceuticals for Human Use (ICH) provides guidelines that are comprehensive sets of recommendations for the development of medicines and the protection of public health. They cover topics such as:

Quality Guidelines:

These include pivotal milestones such as the conduct of stability studies, defining relevant thresholds for impurities testing, and a more scientific and well researched approach to pharmaceutical quality based on Good Manufacturing Practice (GMP) risk management.

Safety Guidelines:

ICH has produced a comprehensive set of safety guidelines to uncover potential risks like carcinogenicity, genotoxicity, and reprotoxicity.

Efficacy Guidelines:

These are concerned with the design, conduct, safety, and reporting of clinical trials. It also covers novel types of medicines derived from biotechnological processes and the use of pharmacogenetics/genomics techniques to produce better-targeted medicines.

Multidisciplinary Guidelines:

These are the cross-cutting topics which do not fit uniquely into one of the Quality, Safety, and Efficacy categories.

The importance of ICH guidelines for pharmaceutical professionals lies in their ability to streamline the development and registration processes for pharmaceutical products, facilitating global acceptance of data and reducing the need for duplicate testing or unnecessary delays in the approval of new drugs. They also provide clarity on the data and evidence needed to support regulatory submissions and meet regulatory expectations.

Furthermore, they promote public health through international harmonization, which contributes to the prevention of unnecessary duplication of clinical trials and post-market clinical evaluations, development and manufacturing of new medicines, registration and supervision of new medicines, and reduction of unnecessary animal testing without compromising safety and effectiveness.

Let's understand and explore how to navigate ICH website to refer to the ICH guidelines, resources and latest updates.

A. Referring to the ICH Quality Guidelines:

1. Opening the Page:

- Open your web browser.

- Type in the URL:

    https://www.ich.org/page/ich-guidelines or simply click on the link or scan QR Code.

- Following page will appear.

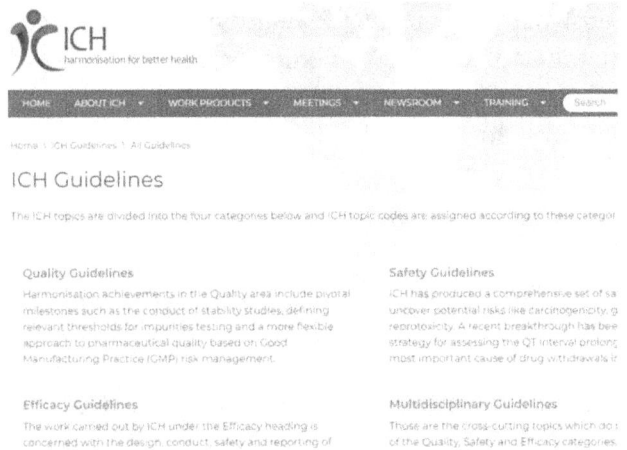

- Click on the types of guidance you want to refer or download.

2. Understanding the Page Layout:

- Let's see one example by exploring the quality guideline.

- Click on the Quality Guidelines. It will navigate you on the page,

  https://www.ich.org/page/quality-guidelines
  Or Scan QR Code

The Pharmaceutical Guidance Navigator

Following is the page layout.

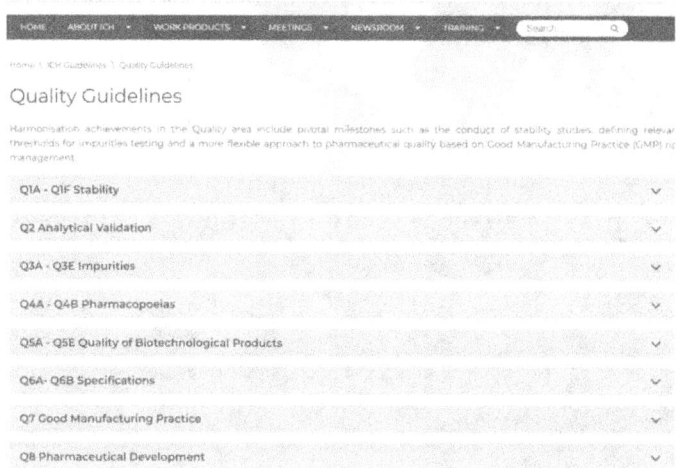

- You can select the tab for which you want to refer to the guidance.

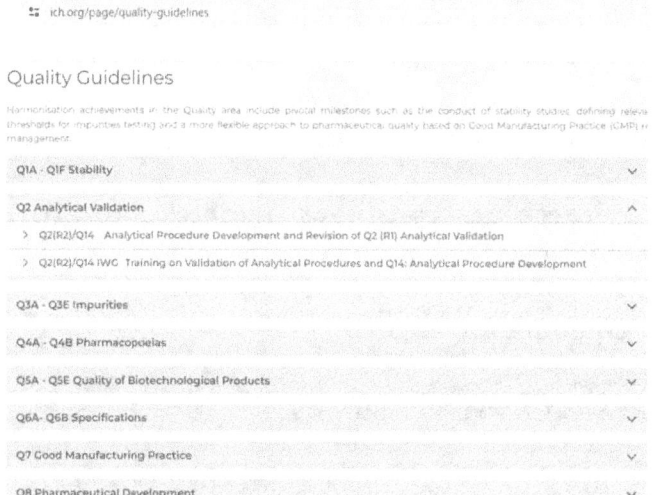

- Furthermore, you can narrow down the selection to navigate the required document. It will give full details regarding the document as well as provide the link of documents to download. Refer to the following screenshot.

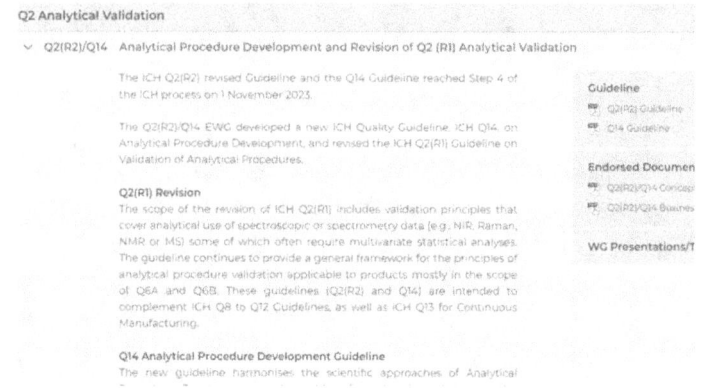

3. Searching for Specific Guidelines:

- If you're looking for a specific guideline, you can use the search function at the top of the page. Enter keywords related to the guideline you're looking for, such as the guideline name or the subject matter.

B. Searching for new updates on ICH Guidelines:

1. Opening the Page:

- Open your web browser.

- Type in the URL:

  https://www.ich.org/page/news or simply click on the link or scan QR code.

2. Understanding the Page Layout:

- The page you see is a list of news items. Each row in the list is a different news item.

- Each news item has a Date, News Title, and News Excerpt. The Date tells you when the news item was posted. The News Title tells you what the news item is about. The News Excerpt gives you a brief summary of the news item.

- Refer to the following screenshot.

The Pharmaceutical Guidance Navigator

News

This section includes news related to ICH.

---

4 March 2024
ICH Q12 IWG "Regulatory and Technical Considerations for Pharmaceutical Product Lifecycle Management"

The ICH Secretariat is pleased to announce the publication of the ICH Q12 "Regulatory and Technical Considerations for Pharmaceutical Product Lifecycle Management Introductory Video" following the publication of the ICH Q12 Module 8 in February 2024.

21 February 2024
The ICH E2D(R1) draft Guideline presently now on the ICH website

The ICH E2D(R1) draft Guideline on "Post-A Definitions and Standards for Managemer Individual Case Safety Reports (ICSRs)" rea ICH Process in February 2024 and entered period.

Chapter 7: Pharmaceutical Inspection Co-operation Scheme (PIC/S) Guidance

The Pharmaceutical Inspection Co-operation Scheme (PIC/S) plays a crucial role in the field of pharmaceuticals. Here are some of its key contributions of PIC/S to the Pharmaceutical community:

Harmonization of Standards:

PIC/S aims to harmonize inspection procedures worldwide by developing common standards in the field of Good Manufacturing Practice (GMP).

Training Opportunities:

It provides training opportunities to inspectors, enhancing their skills and knowledge.

Facilitating Cooperation:

PIC/S facilitates cooperation and networking between competent authorities, regional and international organizations, thus increasing mutual confidence.

Promotion of Quality Assurance:

The scheme promotes quality assurance of inspections and provides a framework for the necessary exchange of information and experience.

Improvement and Harmonization of Technical Standards:

PIC/S continues common efforts towards the improvement and harmonization of technical standards and procedures regarding the inspection of the manufacture of medicinal products.

Global Harmonization:

It extends cooperation to other competent authorities having the national arrangements necessary to apply equivalent standards and procedures, contributing to global harmonization.

In summary, PIC/S guidance is essential in ensuring the quality, safety, and efficacy of medicinal products through harmonized standards, mutual confidence, and global cooperation.

Want to find PIC/S guidelines, resources, and stay up-to-date on the latest regulations? Let's dive into navigating the PIC/S website!

A. Referring to the PICS Guidelines:

1. Opening the Page:

- Launch your preferred web browser.

- Enter the URL:

- https://picscheme.org/en/publications or simply click on the link or scan QR code.

It will open the following page.

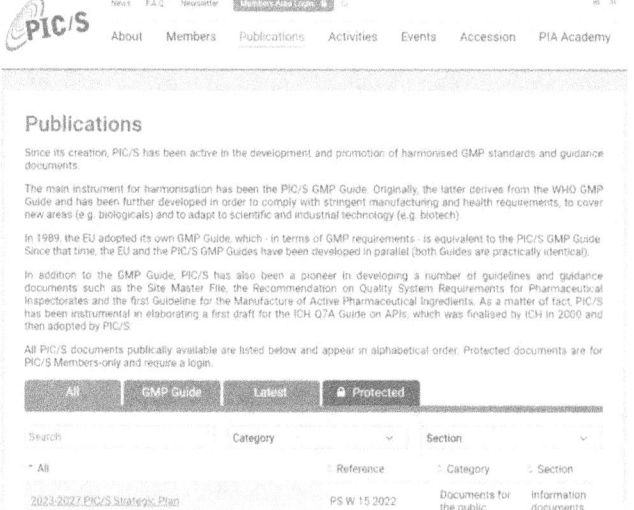

2. Understanding the Page Layout:

- The page you land on is a comprehensive list of various publications related to pharmaceutical inspection and good manufacturing practices. Each row in the list represents a different document.

- Each document has a Title, Category, Section, and reference number. The Title gives you a brief idea of the document's content. The Category and Section provide context about the document's relevance within the broader scheme of pharmaceutical inspection.

3. Navigating the List:

You can scroll through the list to view the documents. The list is organized by the document Title, with the most recent documents appearing at the top.

4. Reading a Document:

To read a document, click on the Title link in the row of the document you are interested in. This will open the document in a new tab, allowing you to read or download it.

5. Searching for Specific Documents:

If you're looking for a specific document, you can use the search function located at the top of the page. Enter keywords related to the document you're looking for, such as the document title or the subject matter. For example, I have entered a keyword 'GMP', it provided all the titles having related keywords in the title. Refer to the following example.

6. Protected Documents:

Some documents are protected and only accessible to PIC/S Members. To access these documents, you'll need to log in with your member credentials.

B. Searching for updates on PICS Guidelines:

1. Opening the Page:

- Open your web browser.

- Type in the URL:

https://picscheme.org/en/news or simply click on the link or scan QR code.

It will open the following page.

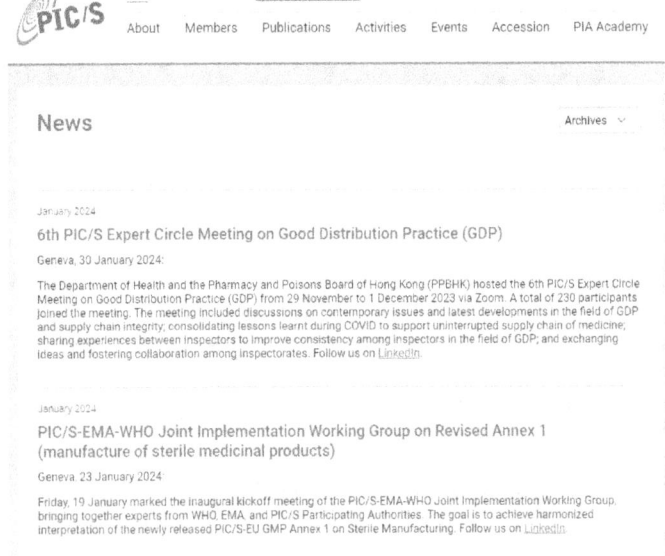

2. Understanding the Page Layout:

- The page you land on is a list of news items related to the Pharmaceutical Inspection Co-operation Scheme (PIC/S). Each news item is represented by a card with a title, date, and brief description.

- The news items are arranged in chronological order, with the most recent news at the top. You can visit the page regularly to check if any new document or guidance has been published by the PIC/S that is relevant for you to know.

3. Navigating the List:

You can scroll through the list to view the news items. If you want to read the previously published news items, you can use the "Archives" dropdown and select the year of news to read the respective year's news.

Chapter 8: World Health Organization (WHO) Guidance

The World Health Organization (WHO) plays a critical role in setting standards for the pharmaceutical industry. Their guidelines are important for several reasons:

Quality Guidelines: WHO guidelines outline good manufacturing practices (GMP) that pharmaceutical companies are advisable to follow. GMPs ensure that medications are produced consistently and meet specific quality standards. This reduces the risk of contamination and ensures patients receive medications with the correct dosage.

Safety and efficacy: WHO guidelines emphasize the importance of ensuring that drugs are safe and effective for their intended use. This helps to protect patients from harmful medications and ensures they receive treatments with proven benefits.

Global harmonization: WHO guidelines provide a common framework for drug development, manufacturing, and regulation. This helps to streamline the process for pharmaceutical companies bringing new drugs to market worldwide.

Informing national regulations: Many countries use WHO guidelines as a foundation for their own national regulations. This helps to ensure a consistent level of quality and safety for medications around the world.

WHO publishes guidelines as Technical Report Series or TRS. It's a publication series from the World Health Organization (WHO) that includes the WHO guidelines for pharmaceuticals, among many other topics.

Think of it like a library with different books on various health-related subjects. In this library, the TRS series is a specific section dedicated to technical reports, and within that section, there are books (reports) on WHO guidelines for pharmaceuticals. Each guideline has a specific TRS number.

In summary, WHO guidance is a helpful resource for the pharmaceutical industry to develop, manufacture, and distribute safe, effective, and high-quality medications.

Let's explore and dive into navigating the WHO website!

A. Referring to the WHO Guidelines:

1. Opening the Page:

- Open your web browser.

- Type in the URL:

  https://www.who.int/teams/health-product-and-policy-standards/standards-and-specifications/norms-and-standards-for-pharmaceuticals/guidelines or simply click on the link or scan QR code.

It will open the following page.

2. Understanding the Page Layout:

- The page you land on is a comprehensive list of guidelines related to the norms and standards for pharmaceuticals. Each guideline is represented by a card with a title and brief description.

- The guidelines are arranged into several categories as follows:

  - Production
  - Quality control
  - Prequalification
  - Regulatory standards
  - Development
  - Distribution
  - Inspections
  - Quality Assurance

3. Navigating the List:

- You can scroll through the list to view the guidelines. If there are more guidelines than can fit on one page, you can navigate to other pages using the navigation link. Refer to the following example of production guidelines.

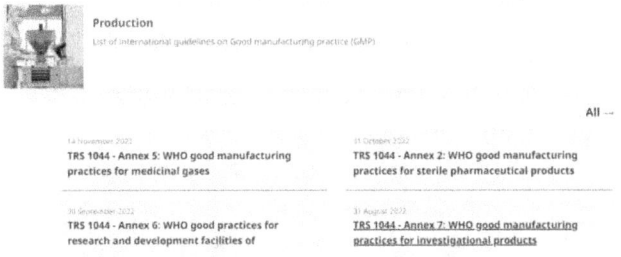

- The page provides a title of guideline, TRS number and date of publication that help you understand which one is the latest one.

- Randomly searching the guideline on a search engine will give multiple links of mainly pdf guidelines and it is very hard to identify which one is the correct one to refer to.

- This method of navigating the WHO guideline will help you identify the correct version of the guideline that you are looking for.

4. **Reading a Guideline:**

To read a guideline, click on the title of the guideline. This will take you to a page where you can refer or download full text of the guideline.

5. Searching for Specific Guidelines:

If you're looking for a specific guideline, you can use the search function located at the top of the page. Enter keywords related to the guideline you're looking for, such as the guideline title or a relevant topic.

Chapter 9: Medicines and Healthcare products Regulatory Agency (MHRA) Guidance

The Medicines and Healthcare products Regulatory Agency (MHRA) is an agency of the UK government that regulates medicines, medical devices, and blood components for transfusion. It plays a vital role in ensuring that the UK's healthcare system operates safely, effectively, and in the best interests of patients.

For the pharmaceutical industry, and specifically for pharmaceutical manufacturers, the MHRA is important for the following reasons:

Regulation and Safety: The MHRA ensures the safety and effectiveness of medicines and medical devices. It provides robust regulation, guidance, and support, helping to safeguard public health.

Promotion of Innovation: By providing expert knowledge, guidance, and experience, the MHRA helps to promote innovation and access to new treatments.

Support for Manufacturers: The MHRA provides guidance for industry and organizations, including manufacturers of biological medicines. This includes guidance on clinical trials, devices, importing and exporting, IT systems, legislation, licensing, and pharmacovigilance.

In summary, the MHRA plays an important role in the pharmaceutical industry by ensuring the safety and efficacy of medicines and medical devices, promoting innovation, and providing support and guidance to manufacturers. It helps manufacturers navigate the regulatory landscape, thereby facilitating the development and marketing of new medicines.

Let's explore an official online platform that is maintained by MHRA.

A. Referring to the MHRA Guidelines:

1. Opening the Page:

- Open your web browser.

- Type in the URL:

    https://www.gov.uk/guidance/good-manufacturing-practice-and-good-distribution-practice or simply click on the link or scan QR code.

The Pharmaceutical Guidance Navigator

You can see the following page.

2. Understanding the Page Layout and Navigating the Page:

- The page you land on is a guidance document related to Good Manufacturing Practice (GMP) and Good Distribution Practice (GDP).

- The page is divided into several sections that are helpful for the pharmaceutical manufacturer and distributor in various aspects.

- You can scroll through the page to view the

different sections.

- Each section has a title and a brief description or list of points related to the title.

- Some sections have links to other pages for more detailed information.

- The page shall navigate to different sections of guidance, examples are summarized below:

    - Guidelines of Good Manufacturing Practice (GMP) and Good Distribution Practice (GDP)

    - Links to the guidance published by MHRA and the European Medicines Agency (EMA) on GMP and GDP including official book of MHRA guidance, Orange Guide: Rules and Guidance for Pharmaceutical Manufacturers and Distributors.

    - Types of inspection

    - Complete a compliance report

    - The inspection

    - Grading of inspection findings

    - Actions after the inspection

- Feedback from GMP inspections
- Suspension of your license
- Transitional Qualified Persons (QPs) for investigational medicinal products (IMPs)
- Fees for inspection

3. **Reading a Section:**

- To read the sections, simply scroll to that section and read the information provided.
- If there is a link for more information, you can click on the link. This will take you to a page with more detailed information.

4. **Searching for Specific Information:**

- If you're looking for specific information, you can use the search function located at the top of the page. Enter keywords related to the information you're looking for, such as "inspection" or "compliance report".

B. Referring to the MHRA Inspectorate Blog:

This blog is a valuable resource for pharmaceutical professionals for several reasons:

1. **Regulatory Updates:** The blog provides the

latest changes in regulatory thinking, guidance, and requirements. This helps professionals stay updated with the evolving landscape of pharmaceutical regulations.

2. **Insights from Inspectors and Managers:** The blog features updates from inspectors and managers at the Medicines and Healthcare products Regulatory Agency (MHRA). These insights can provide a unique perspective on the industry's workings.

3. **Stakeholder Engagement:** The blog serves as a platform for engaging with stakeholders. It invites comments and feedback, fostering a dialogue that can lead to improved practices and policies.

4. **Quality Assurance:** The MHRA Inspectorate's mission is to ensure the availability and quality of medicines. By following the blog, professionals can gain a better understanding of the standards and processes involved in achieving this mission.

5. **Inspection Practices:** The blog can provide insights into the inspection practices for UK manufacturers, wholesale dealers, importers of medicines, clinical trials, and toxicology laboratories. This knowledge can be beneficial for those involved in these areas.

By observing the blog's participation guidelines and

moderation policy, professionals can engage in meaningful discussions and contribute to the pharmaceutical community's growth and development.

Let's explore an official MHRA Inspectorate blog which is online platform that is maintained by MHRA.

1. Opening the Page:

- Open your web browser. Type in the URL: https://mhrainspectorate.blog.gov.uk/ or simply click on the link or scan QR code.

You will see the following page.

2. Understanding the Page Layout:

- The page you land on is the home page of the MHRA Inspectorate Blog. It contains a list of blog posts related to the Medicines and Healthcare products Regulatory Agency (MHRA) Inspectorate.

- Each blog post is represented by a card with a title, date, and brief description.

- The blog posts are arranged in chronological order, with the most recent post at the top.

3. Navigating the List:

- You can scroll through the list to view the blog posts.

- To read a blog post, click on the title of the post. This will take you to a page with the full text of the blog post.

4. Searching for Specific Blog Posts:

If you're looking for a specific blog post, you can use the search function located at the top of the page. Enter keywords related to the blog post you're looking for, such as the title or a relevant topic.

C. Navigating MHRA certificates:

For any organization intending to manufacture and distribute products within the UK market, or seeking to utilize Good Manufacturing Practice (GMP) services such as contract testing, it is imperative to possess the relevant certification from the Medicines and Healthcare products Regulatory Agency (MHRA).

If you are a Marketing Authorization Holder or Contract Giver, who manufactures or supplies healthcare products in the UK, it is crucial to monitor the approval and compliance status of your facilities.

You can refer to the MHRA's official page (https://cms.mhra.gov.uk/mhra/gmp)

and other associated links to download the necessary certificates. These resources will provide insights into the site approval status, which is vital for maintaining business continuity and ensuring the uninterrupted supply of healthcare products in the UK market.

1. **Opening the Page:**

   - Open your web browser. Type in the URL: https://cms.mhra.gov.uk/mhra/gmp or simply click on the link or scan QR code.

You can see the following page.

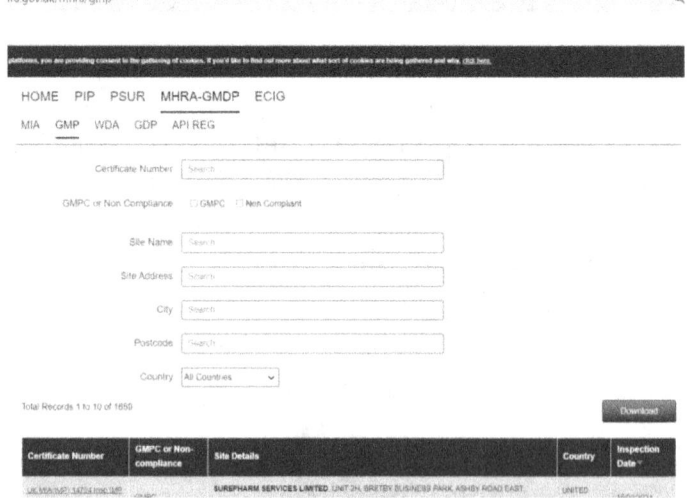

2. Understanding the Page Layout:

- The page you land on is a comprehensive list of Good Manufacturing Practice (GMP) certificates and non-compliance reports issued by the Medicines and Healthcare products Regulatory Agency (MHRA).

- Top of the page has a custom search option and beneath that there is a list.

- Each entry in the list represents a different site, with details such as the Certificate Number, GMPC or Non-compliance, Site Details, Country, and Inspection Date.

3. Navigating the List:

- You can scroll through the list to view the entries. The list is organized by the inspection date, with the most recent inspections at the top.

- If there are more entries than can fit on one page, you can navigate to other pages using the pagination controls at the bottom of the page.

4. Reading an Entry:

To refer to the specific company certificate, you can simply look at the details provided in the row of the entry you are interested in and by clicking on the link of specific Certificate Number.

5. Searching for Specific Entries:

- If you're looking for a specific entry, you can use the search function located at the top of the page. Enter keywords related to the entry you're looking for, such as the site name or country.

- For example, I click on Sandoz Limited, the list will populate all the certificates issued to the Sandoz Limited across all the country. You can further filter it by giving fields to view specific certificates.

The Pharmaceutical Guidance Navigator

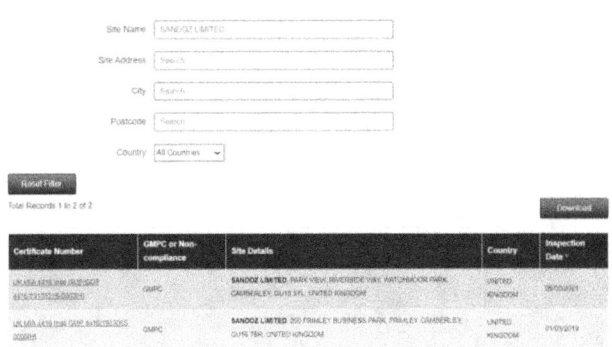

- You can open a specific certificate and also download it for your reference.

The Pharmaceutical Guidance Navigator

Chapter 10: United States Pharmacopeia (USP) News and Updates

The "New and Updated Notices" section of the USP-NF (United States Pharmacopeia–National Formulary) website is useful for pharmaceutical professionals for several reasons:

Updates on Monographs: The page provides new notices on pending monographs. Monographs are standards that describe the necessary quality of a drug substance or product including its intended use, ingredients, and testing methods. Keeping up with these updates helps professionals ensure their products meet the latest standards.

Revision Notices: The page also posts notices of intent to revise certain standards. These notices allow professionals to anticipate changes and adjust their practices accordingly.

General Announcements: The page includes

general announcements about the USP-NF's standards-setting initiatives.

Feedback Opportunities: The page often posts notices requesting user input on various topics. This gives professionals the opportunity to contribute their expertise to the development of standards.

In summary, this page is a valuable resource for pharmaceutical professionals to stay informed about the latest updates, revisions, and announcements related to pharmaceutical standards. It also provides opportunities for professionals to contribute to the standards-setting process.

Referring to the USP updates:

1. Opening the Page:

- Open your web browser.

- Type in the URL:

    https://www.uspnf.com/notices/new   or simply click on the link or scan QR code.

You can see the following page.

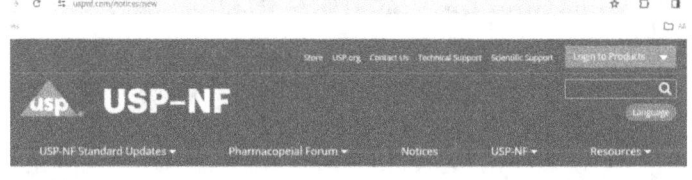

2. Understanding the Page Layout:

- The page you land on is a list of new notices related to the United States Pharmacopeia and the National Formulary (USP-NF). Each notice is represented by a title, brief description and date.

- The notices are arranged in chronological order, with the most recent notices at the top.

3. Navigating the List:

You can scroll through the list to view the notices.

4. Reading a Notice:

To read a notice, click on the title of the notice. This will take you to a page with the full text of the notice, along with any associated images or documents.

5. Searching for Specific Notices:

If you're looking for a specific notice, you can use the search function located at the top of the page. Enter keywords related to the notice you're looking for, such as the notice title or a relevant topic.

In addition to the news and updates on the website, you can navigate to the website using the navigation bars, viz, USP-NF Standard Updates, Pharmacopeial Forum, Notices, USP-NF, and Resources. The website provides valuable resources and updates for pharmaceutical professionals.

Chapter 11: European Directorate for the Quality of Medicines & Healthcare (EDQM) Guidance

The European Directorate for the Quality of Medicines & HealthCare (EDQM) is a leading organization that protects public health by enabling the development, supporting the implementation, and monitoring the application of quality standards for safe medicines and their safe use. Here's how it can be helpful for pharmaceutical professionals:

Development of Quality Standards: The EDQM enables the development of quality standards for medicines. These standards, recognized as a scientific benchmark worldwide, ensure the quality and safety of medicines.

Monitoring Application of Standards: The EDQM monitors the application of these quality standards. This helps in maintaining the quality of medicines and ensuring their safe use.

Supporting Implementation of Standards: The EDQM supports the implementation of these quality standards. This ensures that the standards are effectively applied in the production of medicines.

Providing Updates and News: The EDQM website provides updates and news related to medicines and healthcare. This helps pharmaceutical professionals stay informed about the latest developments in the field.

Offering Training and Events: The EDQM organizes events and training sessions. These provide opportunities for professionals to learn and enhance their skills.

Publishing Scientific Texts: The EDQM oversees and coordinates the production of high-quality scientific texts. These texts can be a valuable resource for pharmaceutical professionals.

In summary, the EDQM plays a crucial role in ensuring the quality and safety of medicines. It provides pharmaceutical professionals with the resources and support they need to produce safe and effective medicines. It also offers opportunities for learning and professional development.

Referring to the EDQM updates:

1. **Opening the Page:**

   - Open your web browser.

- Type in the URL:

  https://www.edqm.eu/en/edqm/about/newsroom or simply click on the link or scan QR code.

It will open the following page.

2. **Understanding the Page Layout:**

- The page you land on is a list of news items related to the European Directorate for the

Quality of Medicines & HealthCare (EDQM). Each news item is represented by a card with a title, date, and brief description.

- The news items are arranged in chronological order, with the most recent news at the top.

3. Navigating the List:

You can scroll through the list to view the news items. If there are more news items than can fit on one page, you can navigate to other pages.

4. Reading a News Item:

To read a news item, click on the title of the news item. This will take you to a page with the full text of the news item, along with any associated images or documents.

5. Searching for Specific News Items:

If you're looking for a specific news item, you can use the search function located at the top of the page. Enter keywords related to the news item you're looking for, such as the news item title or a relevant topic.

Chapter 12: European Union (EU) Good Manufacturing Practice (GMP) Guidance

In this section, we will talk about two websites, https://health.ec.europa.eu/index_en and https://www.ema.europa.eu/en/homepage. Both are related to health and medicine within the European Union, but they serve different purposes:

European Commission Public Health (https://health.ec.europa.eu/index_en):

This is a department of the European Commission responsible for EU policy on food safety and health, and for monitoring the implementation of related laws. Their mission is to make Europe a healthier and safer place by building a strong European Health Union to protect and improve public health, ensure Europe's food is sustainable and safe, protect the health and welfare of farm animals, and protect the health of crops and forests. They achieve their goals by monitoring, listening to concerns, and taking action.

European Medicines Agency

(https://www.ema.europa.eu/en/homepage):

The EMA is an agency of the European Union responsible for the scientific evaluation, supervision, and safety monitoring of medicines. They work to ensure that all medicines available on the EU market are safe, effective, and of high quality. The EMA serves a community of people living in the EU.

A. EU GMP Search for Guidance Documents:

1. Opening the Page:

- Open your web browser.

- Type in the URL:

  https://health.ec.europa.eu/medicinal-products/eudralex_en or simply click on the link or scan QR code.

  You can see the following page. On this page, you will get the information on EU legislation and procedures for the regulation of human medicines, volumes 1-4 and 9-10 of the rules governing medicinal products in the EU

- Guidelines for good manufacturing practices for medicinal products for human and veterinary use are provided in Volume 4. To access that, type in the URL: https://health.ec.europa.eu/medicinal-products/eudralex/eudralex-volume-4_en or simply click on the link or scan QR code.

You can see the following page.

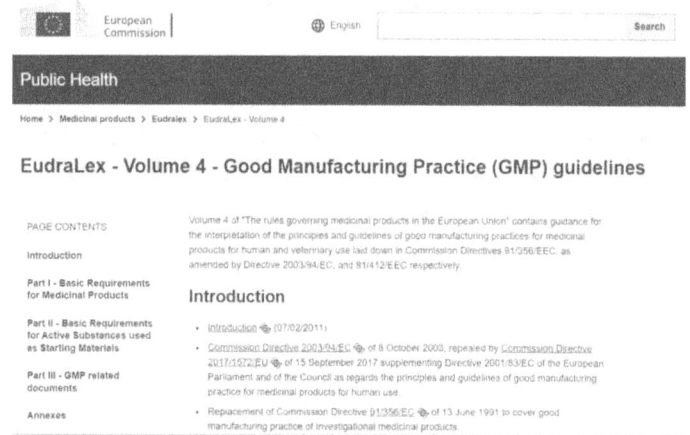

This page provides you the mandatory guidelines that are required to be followed while manufactured medicinal formulations are intended to market in the European region or governed using the European region guidelines.

2. Understanding the Page Layout:

- The page you land on is a guidance document related to Good Manufacturing Practice (GMP) for medicinal products for human and veterinary use.

- The page is divided into several sections, each dealing with a specific aspect of GMP.

3. Navigating the Page:

- You can scroll through the page to view the different sections.

- Each section has a title and a brief description or list of points related to the title.

- All the sections have links to relevant pages or documents for more detailed information either in the webpage form or PDF document that you can download for offline use.

4. Searching for Specific Information:

If you're looking for specific information, you can use the search function located at the top of the page. Enter keywords related to the information you're looking for, such as "Good Manufacturing Practices" or "Good Distribution Practices".

5. Understanding the Sections:

The sections provide detailed information about different aspects of GMP, including introduction, basic requirements for medicinal products, basic requirements for active substances used as starting materials, GMP related documents, annexes, glossary, GMP requirements for Advanced Therapy Medicinal Products, and other documents related to GMP and GDP.

B. Search for latest updates on https://health.ec.europa.eu:

1. Opening the Page:

- Open your web browser.

- Type in the URL:

  https://health.ec.europa.eu/medicinal-products/latest-updates_en or simply click on the link or scan QR code.

You can see the following page.

Public Health

Home > Medicinal products > Latest updates

Medicinal products - Latest updates

Filter by | Medicinal products - Latest updates (313)

Keywords

[Search] [Clear filters]

Showing results 1 to 20

News announcement | 20 March 2024
Global Gateway: European Commission and Belgian Presidency increase their support to the African Medicines Agency
Global Gateway: European Commission and Belgian Presidency increase their support to the African Medicines Agency

News announcement | 12 March 2024
Commission proposes new measures for the better lifecycle management of medicine authorisations
Commission proposes new measures for the better lifecycle management of medicine authorisations

2. Understanding the Page Layout:

- The page you land on is the home page of the Latest Updates for Medicinal Products. It contains a list of updates related to medicinal products.

- Each update is represented by a card with a title, date, and brief description.

- The updates are arranged in chronological order, with the most recent update at the top.

3. Navigating the List:

- You can scroll through the list to view the updates.

- To read an update, click on the title of the update. This will take you to a page with the full text of the update.

4. Searching for Specific Updates:

If you're looking for a specific update, you can use the search function located at the top of the page. Enter keywords related to the update you're looking for, such as the title or a relevant topic.

C. Referring to the European Medicines Agency Guidance:

1. **Opening the Page:**

- Open your web browser.

- Type in the URL:

  https://www.ema.europa.eu/en/human-regulatory-overview or simply click on the link or scan QR code.

You can see the following page.

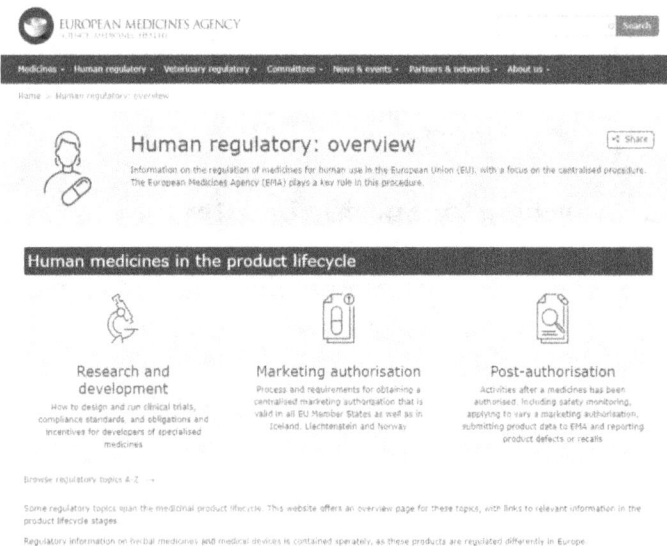

2. Understanding the Page Layout:

- The page you land on is the home page of the Human regulatory: overview. It provides the Information on the regulation of medicines for human use in the European Union (EU), with a focus on the centralised procedure. The European Medicines Agency (EMA) plays a key role in this procedure.

- If you scroll down, you can see the following page with various links that will help you to navigate different guidelines and topics.

ıan-regulatory-overview#ema-inpage-item-38499

Topics A-Z

Accelerated assessment

Adaptive pathways

Advanced therapies

Antimicrobial resistance in human medicine

Biosimilar medicines

Clinical data publication

Compassionate use

Compliance

Conditional marketing authorisation

Coronavirus disease (COVID-19)

Data submission on authorised medicines (Article 57)

Ethical use of animals in medicine testing

Falsified medicines

Fees

Generic and hybrid applications

Medical devices

Medicines for older people

Marketing authorisation

Medicine shortages and availability issues

Medicines for use outside the European Union

Orphan designation: Overview

Paediatric medicines: Overview

Parallel distribution

Pharmacovigilance: Overview

Pharmacovigilance fees

3. Searching for Specific News Items:

If you're looking for a specific news item, you can use the search function located at the top of the page. Enter keywords related to the news item you're looking for, such as the title or a relevant topic.

D. Referring to the European Medicines Agency news:

1. Opening the Page:

- Open your web browser. Type in the URL:

  https://www.ema.europa.eu/en/news or simply click on the link or scan QR code.

You can see the following page.

2. Understanding the Page Layout:

- The page you land on is the home page of the News section. It contains a list of news items related to the European Medicines Agency.

- Each news item is represented by a card with a title, date, and brief description.

- The news items are arranged in chronological order, with the most recent news at the top.

3. Navigating the List:

- You can scroll through the list to view the news items.

- To read a news item, click on the title of the news item. This will take you to a page with the full text of the news item.

4. Searching for Specific News Items:

If you're looking for a specific news item, you can use the search function located at the top of the page. Enter keywords related to the news item you're looking for, such as the title or a relevant topic.

E. Navigating EU GMP Site Classification and Compliance Status:

The European Union relies on individual member

states for inspections and enforcement of EU GMP. Each member state has a National Competent Authority (NCA) responsible for overseeing pharmaceutical manufacturing.

Process:

- Identify the European country where the pharmaceutical company's manufacturing site is located.

- Search for the NCA's website for that specific country. Most NCA websites have an English version. Here are some resources to help you find the relevant NCA:

    https://www.ema.europa.eu/en/partners-networks/eu-partners/eu-member-states/national-competent-authorities-human (European Commission - Directory of the European Union)

- To view certificate details and validity, you need to go to the page https://eudragmdp.ema.europa.eu/inspections/displayHome.do.

The Pharmaceutical Guidance Navigator

- Once you click on the page, it will display the following.

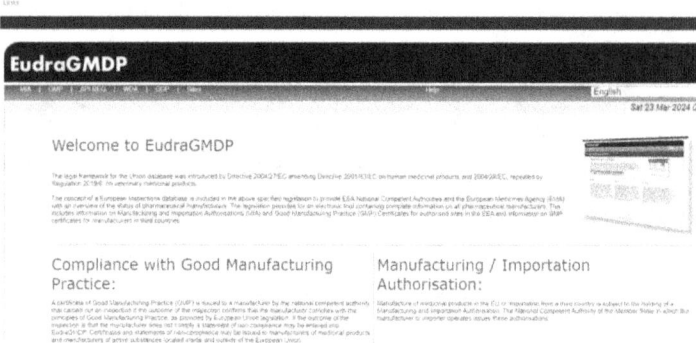

- On the top left, you can see the links, as MIA | GMP | API REG | WDA | GDP | Sites. Select the link that you are interested in. For example, if you want to search for a GMP certificate of any organization, click on the GMP. It will display the following.

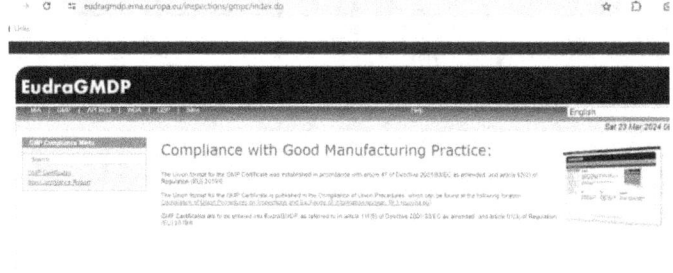

- Click on the GMP certificate link available on the left side of the page. You will see the following page.

- It will open the following page.

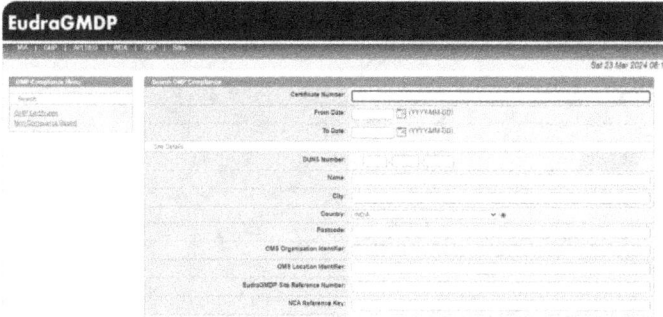

- Provide suitable details, for example, write initial few words of company name under the heading Name. The selection of a country is mandatory to search for the certificates. Click of the Search button and it will give list of certificates with following details:

  o Certificate Number

- EudraGMDP Document Reference Number
- Document Type
- MIA Number
- OMS Organisation Identifier
- OMS Location Identifier
- Site Name
- Site Address
- City
- Postcode
- Country
- Inspection End Date

By following these steps, you should be able to identify a company's EU GMP site classification and compliance status. Remember, this information can be crucial for making informed decisions regarding the quality and safety of pharmaceutical products.

Chapter 13: Therapeutic Goods Administration (TGA) Guidance (Australia)

The Australian Therapeutic Goods Administration (TGA) offers important guidance for pharmaceutical professionals. The guidance will be helpful when the manufacturer or sponsor is intended to produce or supply the product to the Australian market. Their resources include:

Prescription Medicines Registration: Guidelines for registering new medicines or modifying existing ones.

Manufacturing Guidance: Ensures medicine manufacturing meets required standards.

Specific Technical Requirements: Information on additional requirements for different medicine types.

Advertising Guidance: Ensures advertising

complies with regulations.

Regular Updates: The TGA keeps its guidance current with industry changes.

A. Exploring TGA Guidance Documents:

1. Opening the Page:

- Open your web browser. Type in the URL:

  https://www.tga.gov.au/resources or simply click on the link or scan QR code.

You can see the following page.

2. Understanding the Page Layout:

- The page you land on is the home page of the Resources section. It contains a list of resources related to therapeutic goods.

- The page provides the following information.

  - Frequently Searched in Resources

  - Resources and Publications

    Resources: Search resources for guidance, checklists, international scientific guidelines, compositional guidelines, and forms.

    Guidance: Therapeutic Goods Administration (TGA) guidance for industry.

    Forms: Therapeutic Goods Administration (TGA) forms.

    Checklists: Therapeutic Goods Administration (TGA) checklists.

    Publications: Find corporate publications, reports, statements, labeling exemptions, and stakeholder surveys.

> Decision Trees: Use decision trees to work out classifications, advertising and manufacturing questions, and product types.

- Application and Enquiry Portals and Reference Information for Applications

- Safety, Shortages, and How to Make a Report

- Australian Register of Therapeutic Goods, and Cancellations and Suspensions

- Prescription Medicine Decisions

- Regulatory Notices

- Regulatory compliance and actions

- Sponsors

• Since we are discussing guidelines and resources for industry to update themselves, the section, Resources and Publications is useful pages to refer to get required guidance and documents to refer.

3. Reading a Resource:

To read a resource, click on the title of the resource. This will take you to a page with the full text of the resource, along with any associated images or documents.

4. Searching for Specific Resources:

If you're looking for a specific resource, you can use the search function located at the top of the page. Enter keywords related to the resource you're looking for, such as the title or a relevant topic.

5. Referring to the international guidelines adopted by TGA.

- In Australia, international scientific guidelines are also followed to help sponsors comply with legislative requirements. The Therapeutic Goods Administration (TGA) in Australia strives to align its regulatory approaches to therapeutic products with those of similar international regulatory bodies.

- You can refer to guidelines adopted by TGA at, https://www.tga.gov.au/resources/resource/international-scientific-guidelines.

B. Search for latest updates on TGA website:

1. Opening the Page:

- Open your web browser. Type in the URL:

  https://www.tga.gov.au/news/news or simply click on the link or scan QR code.

  You will see the following page.

Products we regulate   Product safety   How we regulate   Guidance and resources

Home > News and Community

News

Our news gives you the latest on a range of health product safety and quality topics, such as changes to guidelines, fines for fake products and unlawful advertising, industry events and more.

Listen   Print   Share   RSS feed

Read more TGA news in our Media releases.
Trove at the National Library of Australia has copies of archived behind the news articles.

Latest News

Updates to the Prescribing Medicines in Pregnancy database - March 2024
18 March 2024 | News

The Prescription Medicines in Pregnancy database has been updated to include new and amended entries.

2. Understanding the Page Layout:

- The page you land on is the home page of the News section. It contains a list of news items related to the Therapeutic Goods Administration.

- Each news item is represented by a card with a title, date, and brief description.

- The news items are arranged in chronological order, with the most recent news at the top.

3. Navigating the List:

- You can scroll through the list to view the news items.

- To read a news item, click on the title of the news item. This will take you to a page with the full text of the news item.

4. Searching for Specific News Items:

If you're looking for a specific news item, you can use the search function located at the top of the page. Enter keywords related to the news item you're looking for, such as the title or a relevant topic.

C. Navigating Australian Register of Therapeutic Goods (ARTG):

The Australian Register of Therapeutic Goods (ARTG), managed by the Therapeutic Goods Administration (TGA), is an essential resource for pharmaceutical professionals. It serves as a comprehensive database, providing detailed information about therapeutic goods that are authorized for supply in Australia.

The ARTG plays a crucial role in ensuring the legality and safety of therapeutic goods. Unless exempted, any therapeutic goods not listed on the ARTG are prohibited from being supplied in Australia. This helps pharmaceutical professionals to verify the legitimacy of the products they deal with and ensures that they comply with Australian regulations.

It's a factual and regulatory tool, rather than an advisory one, designed to support pharmaceutical professionals in their work. To verify sponsor of medicinal product, device or other applicable products listed by Therapeutic Goods Administration (TGA) in Australia, follow these steps:

1. **Australian Register of Therapeutic Goods (ARTG):**

    - The ARTG is a comprehensive database of therapeutic goods that have been evaluated and approved by the TGA.

    - Open the page,

        https://www.tga.gov.au/products/australian-register-therapeutic-goods-artg/searching-

australian-register-therapeutic-goods-artg.

On this page, you can search using various criteria, such as:

- Product name
- License details
- Sponsor details
- Active ingredient names
- ARTG identifier number

- Also, you can use the ARTG Search Visualisation Tool at <https://compliance.health.gov.au/artg/>

and perform advanced search to drill down the database search to identify valid sponsors for the products.

- Refer to the following screenshot.

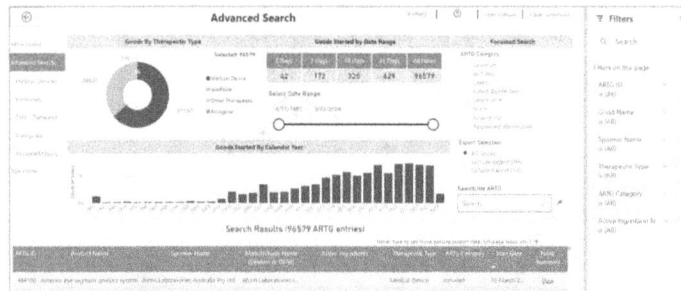

2. Australian Manufacturer Search:

- If you specifically want to verify an Australian manufacturer, you can explore the Australian Manufacturer Search provided by the TGA: Australian Manufacturer Search at https://www.tga.gov.au/resources/australian-manufacturer-search.

- On opening the page, you will see the following page.

The Pharmaceutical Guidance Navigator

Home > Guidance and resources

Australian manufacturer search

A list of Australian manufacturers that hold a current TGA manufacturing licence.

◄• Listen   🖶 Print   ＜ Share

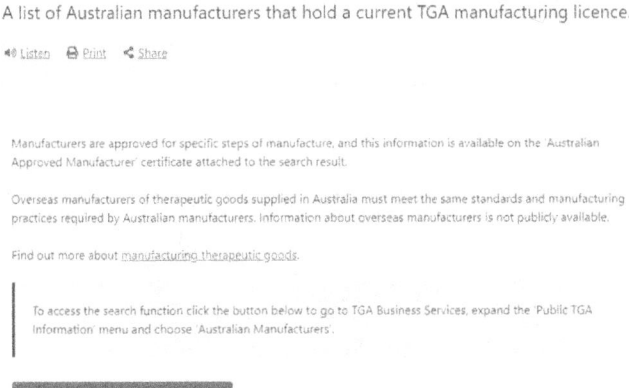

- You can click on the button "Search Australian Manufacturer" and it will navigate you to the following page.

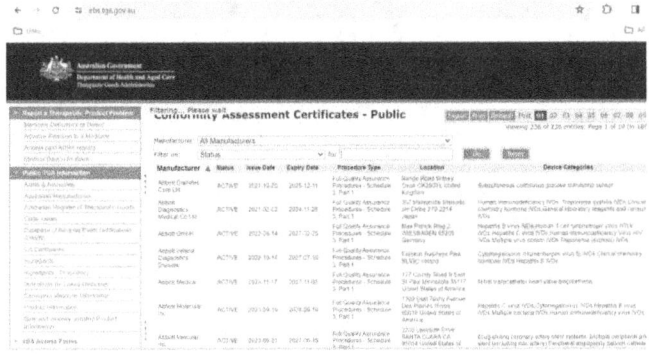

- This search lists Australian manufacturers holding a current TGA manufacturing license. It includes information about the specific steps of manufacture approved for each manufacturer.

- **Permissions and Approvals:**

  o The TGA also maintains databases related to permissions and approvals:

    i. **Section 19A Approvals Database:** Search for approvals to import and supply medicines not in the ARTG to address medicine shortages.

    ii. **Section 14 Consents Database:** Contains consents to import, supply, or export therapeutic goods that do not comply with standards.

    iii. **Advertising Permissions:** Notices of approved and permitted restricted representations.

  o Explore the Permissions and Approvals page, https://www.tga.gov.au/resources/permissions-and-approvals for more details.

- **Bonus tip:**

    o Sometimes it may be difficult to identify and search specific company names on the TGA site. You can use google search with the syntax, [Company name], site:https://www.tga.gov.au/ to search company specific links or pages on TGA site. For example, I want to use details about the company name that starts with Sun Pharma. I wrote in the search bar "Sun Pharma, site:https://www.tga.gov.au/", and it displayed the following.

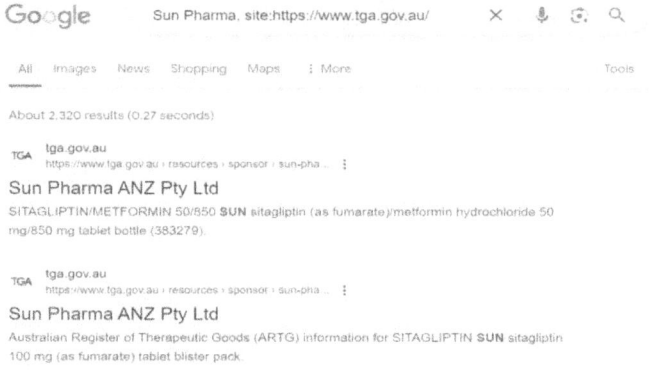

    o You can use this technique for any of the websites to identify specific keywords on a predetermined website.

Chapter 14: Health Canada Guidance

Health Canada offers guidance documents to help pharmaceutical professionals understand regulations and policies. These documents are especially helpful for those distributing pharmaceutical products in Canada.

The guidance documents help you with:

Interpreting regulations: They clarify requirements for good manufacturing practices and other regulations.

Preparing drug submissions: They provide guidance on submitting applications to sell drugs in Canada.

Labeling drugs: There are specific guidelines for labeling pharmaceutical drugs to ensure accurate information.

Quality assurance: The documents guide quality assurance for clinical trials to ensure safe and effective drugs.

Fair and consistent implementation: The documents ensure Health Canada's policies are applied fairly and consistently.

A. Health Canada Search for GMP Guidance Documents:

1. Opening the Page:

- Open your web browser.

- Type in the URL:

    https://www.canada.ca/en/health-canada/services/drugs-health-products/compliance-enforcement/good-manufacturing-practices/guidance-documents.html or simply click on the link or scan QR code.

    You can see the following page.

2. **Understanding the Page Layout**:

- The page you land on is the home page of the Guidance Documents section. It contains a list of guidance documents related to Good Manufacturing Practices (GMP) for drugs and health products.

- Each document is represented by a title.

- The documents are arranged in categories, with each category having its own section.

3. **Navigating the List:**

- You can scroll through the page to view the different categories and documents.

- To read a document, click on the title of the document. This will take you to a page with the full text of the document.

4. Searching for Specific Documents:

- If you're looking for a specific document, you can use the search function located at the top of the page. Enter keywords related to the document you're looking for, such as the title or a relevant topic.

B. Navigating Health Canada for Pharmaceutical Company for Compliance and Enforcement Status

Let's understand here's how to find a company's site Compliance and Enforcement Status with Health Canada:

1. **Understanding Site Classification:**

   - Health Canada doesn't directly assign a "site classification" to pharmaceutical companies. Instead, they focus on compliance with Good Manufacturing Practices (GMP).

2. **Finding Compliance Information:** Here's the process to identify a company's GMP compliance status:

   - **Health Canada Website:** Open the Health Canada website link,

     https://www.canada.ca/en/health-canada/services/drugs-health-products/reports-publications/compliance-enforcement.html.

The Pharmaceutical Guidance Navigator

You will see the following page.

Compliance and Enforcement

As part of its regulatory responsibilities, Health Canada is responsible for compliance monitoring and enforcement activities related to health products in order to verify that regulatory requirements are being applied appropriately.

What information can you find here?

This section contains links to reports and publications related to compliance and enforcement.

- Community Pharmacy Inspection Program Annual Report, Fiscal Year 2019-2020
- Community Pharmacy Inspection Program Annual Report, Fiscal Year 2018-2019
- Community Pharmacy Inspection Program discovers drug diversion in Hamilton pharmacy
- Community Pharmacy Inspection Program Annual Report, Fiscal Year 2017-2018
- Community Pharmacy Inspection Program Annual Report, Fiscal Year 2016-2017
- Community Pharmacy Inspection Program Annual Report, Fiscal Year 2015-2016
- Verifying compliance of health products on the market: April 1, 2015 to March 31, 2016
- Good Clinical Practices - Reports
- Inspectorate Program Annual Inspection Summary Reports
   - 2015 - 2016
   - 2014 - 2015
   - 2013 - 2014
   - 2012 - 2013
- Inspection Tracker: Drug Manufacturing Establishments

- Click on the link of Inspection Tracker: Drug Manufacturing Establishments. It will take you to the page,

https://www.canada.ca/en/health-canada/services/drugs-health-products/reports-publications/compliance-enforcement/inspection-tracker-drug-manufacturing-establishments.html.

You can see the following page.

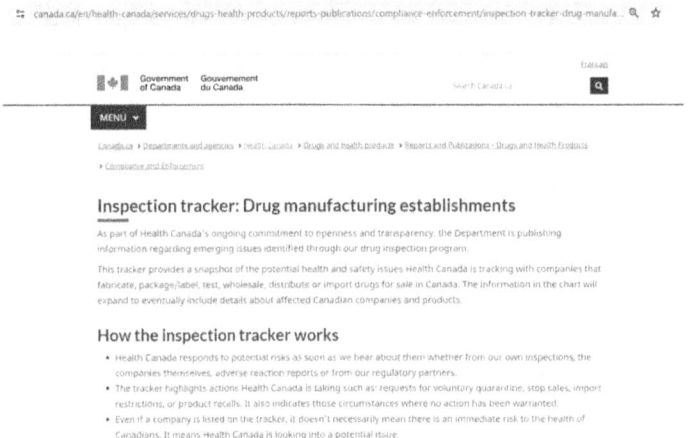

3. **Search for organization:** On this page, the list of organizations inspected by Health Canada is described in two tables. First table is the list of organizations with open items and the second table is the list of organizations with closed items.

- The tables contain information such as Establishment, Status of issue, Source of information under review, and Primary reason for action.

- You can use filters to search the name of an organization available in the table, when all the information is not appearing on one page. You can also filter the table with custom key words such as country name.

- To know how this tracker works, the page has very good explanation under the section "How the inspection tracker works"

- To review the Compliance and enforcement report for Cannabis inspection, you can go to the page link,

  https://www.canada.ca/en/health-canada/services/drugs-medication/cannabis/research-data/compliance-enforcement-report-cannabis-inspection-data-summary/report-links.html

The page will provide the information such as License Holder Name, Province or Territory, Inspection Start Date, Inspection Type, Sampling Conducted, Observations, Inspection Rating, Measures initiated by Health Canada.

Chapter 15: Pharmaceuticals and Medical Devices Agency (PMDA), Japan Guidance

The Pharmaceuticals and Medical Devices Agency (PMDA) of Japan provides guidance that is beneficial to various stakeholders in the pharmaceutical industry. Here's how:

Pharmaceutical Industry: The guidance provided by PMDA is crucial for the development of drugs, medical devices, regenerative medicines, and in vitro diagnostics. It helps the industry understand the regulatory requirements and standards, ensuring the safety and efficacy of their products intended to market in Japan.

Medical Professionals: Medical professionals rely on the PMDA's guidance to understand the safety measures, precautions, and potential adverse effects of various pharmaceutical products. This information is vital for them to make informed decisions about patient care.

In summary, PMDA's guidance plays a crucial role in ensuring the quality, safety, and efficacy of pharmaceutical products, benefiting the industry, and medical professionals.

A. PMDA Search for Japanese GMP Guidance Documents:

1. Opening the Page:

- Open your web browser. Type in the URL:

    https://www.pmda.go.jp/english/review-services/index.html or simply click on the link or scan QR code.

    You can see the following page.

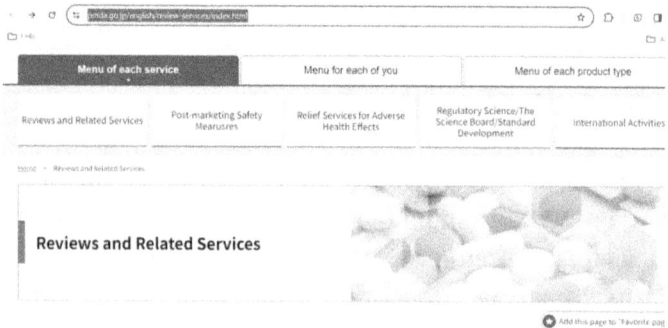

2. Understanding the Page Layout:

- The page you land on is the home page of the Review Services section. It contains a list of services related to the review of pharmaceuticals and medical devices.

- Each service is represented by a card with a title and a brief description.

- The services are arranged in categories, with each category having its own section.

- For example, if you want to read the GMP guidance, hover the cursor on Reviews and Related Services. You will see the following.

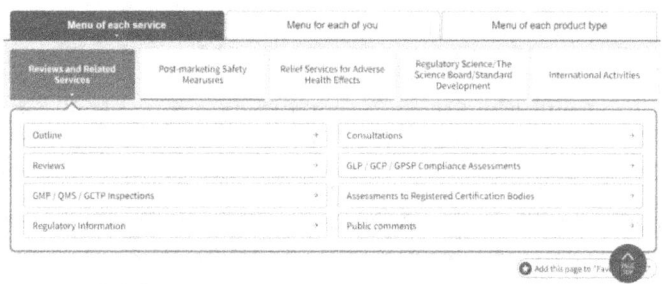

- Further click on the Regulatory information, it will take you to the page,

  https://www.pmda.go.jp/english/review-services/regulatory-info/0002.html.

You can see the link to the guidance as follows.

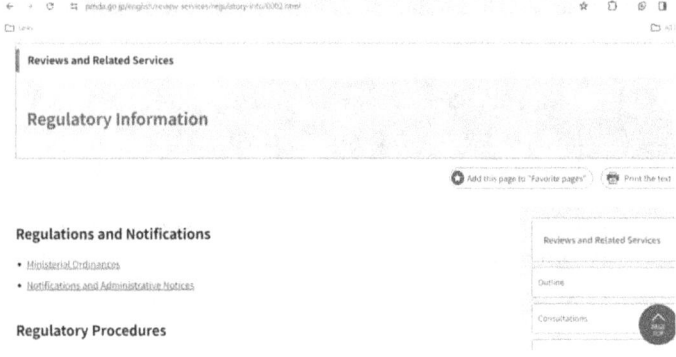

- Click on the link for which you are interested. The links of guidance are available under the various headings such as Regulations and Notifications, Regulatory Procedures, Guidance, and Other Related Information. You can refer and download the required guidance for reading and reference.

- You can directly go to the page,

    https://www.pmda.go.jp/english/review-services/gmp-qms-gctp/0001.html

The Pharmaceutical Guidance Navigator

to refer to the various Regulations and Guidelines and other important documents on the page.

3. Navigating other useful information on the website:

- To refer to the other useful information, you can use the navigation buttons provided at top of the page. Refer to the following screenshot.

- Using the navigation buttons such as Reviews and Related Services, Post-marketing Safety Measures, Relief Services for Adverse Health Effects, Regulatory Science/The Science Board/Standard Development, and International Activities, you can refer to the various useful guidelines.

4. **Searching for Specific Services:**

- If you're looking for specific information, you can use the search function located at the top of the page. Enter keywords related to the service you're looking for, such as the title or a relevant topic.

B. Navigating PMDA's Website for Site Registration Status with the agency

Here's how to find the information you need on the PMDA (Pharmaceuticals and Medical Devices Agency) website:

1. **Search by Establishment Registration Number:**

- Go to the PMDA's "Publication of foreign manufacturer certification/registration number" at page

    https://www.pmda.go.jp/review-services/drug-reviews/foreign-mfr/0003.html.

- This page is in Japanese, but you can use a translation tool of your browser to read in English or any supporting language.

- This page contains two links as displayed below: one for the PDF version and another for the Excel version.

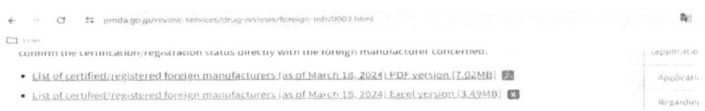

Open the file and search for the company name for which you want to verify the details. The details include such as Applicant Code, Registration Number, Type of Business, Type of Registration, Name, Address, Date of Registration, Expiry Date, etc.

The Pharmaceutical Guidance Navigator

Chapter 16: Agência Nacional de Vigilância Sanitária (ANVISA) - Brazilian Regulations

ANVISA, the Brazilian health regulatory agency, offers valuable guidance for pharmaceutical companies. Their guidance covers key areas like registration, Good Manufacturing Practices (GMP), inspections, and risk assessment.

Following ANVISA's guidelines helps manufacturers in several ways:

Compliance and Market Entry: Understanding regulations ensures smooth registration and market entry for drugs in Brazil.

Quality Assurance: ANVISA's GMP covers various aspects of production, promoting consistent high-quality drug manufacturing.

Inspection Preparation: Pre-inspection information allows companies to prepare well in advance for ANVISA inspections.

Risk Management: ANVISA's risk-based approach to inspections helps manufacturers identify and address potential risks in their operations.

Overall, following ANVISA's guidance leads to improved product quality, patient safety, and business success for pharmaceutical manufacturers willing to distribute the pharmaceutical products in Brazil.

1. **ANVISA Good Manufacturing Practices (GMP):**

    - Open the URL: https://www.gov.br/anvisa/pt-br/english/regulation-of-companies/good-manufacturing-practices in the relevant browser.

    - You can see the following page.

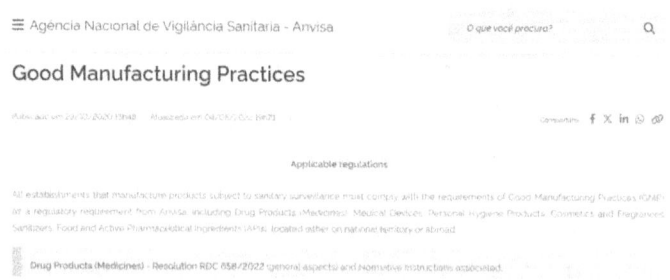

- This webpage provides information on Good Manufacturing Practices (GMP) required by establishments manufacturing products subject to sanitary surveillance by ANVISA. It details the regulations and certifications for GMP compliance.

You can scroll through the page and refer to the various useful guidelines.

The Pharmaceutical Guidance Navigator

Chapter 17: South African Health Products Regulatory Authority (SAHPRA) Regulations

This guide helps you navigate the websites of the South African Health Products Regulatory Authority (SAHPRA) to find relevant information on pharmaceutical regulations, guidance documents, news, and compliance resources.

General Information and News:

- **SAHPRA:** https://www.sahpra.org.za/

is the primary website for SAHPRA and offers a comprehensive overview of their activities. Once you open the website, you will see the following page.

- There are three cards, viz. Forms, Guidelines, Communication to industry, and templates.

- The page, https://www.sahpra.org.za/guidelines/

an entire database of guidelines that is helpful for the pharmaceutical industry professionals. And the page, https://www.sahpra.org.za/guidelines-notice-board/

consist of updates on newly published guidelines.

- The page,

  https://www.sahpra.org.za/communication-to-industry/

  consist of communications done by authority to the industry and useful communication.

- Use the search bar at the top right corner to find specific information.

- You can scroll through the page to get more details about news updates, Databases and Registers.

- You can also refer to the navigation bar and explore the useful information provided on the site.

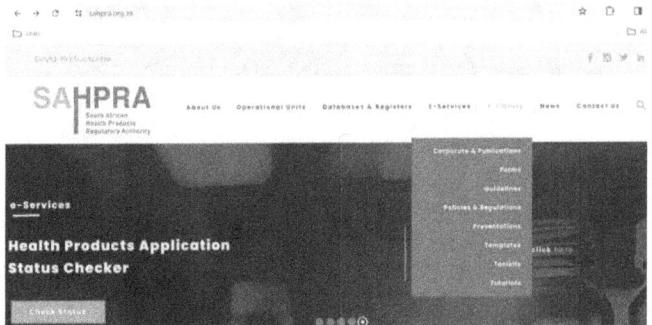

- For monitoring industry news and publications related to South African pharmaceutical regulations, you can refer to the page, https://www.sahpra.org.za/newsroom/.

Chapter 18: Active Pharmaceutical Ingredients Committee (APIC) Guidance

The Active Pharmaceutical Ingredients Committee (APIC) offers several resources to help pharmaceutical manufacturers with quality assurance. These resources include:

- A guide for implementing a Quality Management System (QMS) specific to Active Pharmaceutical Ingredients (APIs).

- A guideline for establishing Quality Agreements between API manufacturers and their customers.

- A practical guide to implementing ICH Q7, a guideline on Good Manufacturing Practice for APIs.

These resources help manufacturers comply with regulations, improve quality assurance processes, and ensure the safety of their products.

1. Opening the Page:

- Open your web browser.

- Type in the URL: https://apic.cefic.org/publications/ or simply click on the link or scan QR code.

- You will see the following page.

2. Understanding the Page Layout:

- The page you land on is the home page of the Publications section. It contains a list of publications related to the Active Pharmaceutical Ingredients Committee (APIC).

- Each publication is represented by a card with a title and a link to read more. On clicking on read more, it will open the page with a link to read and download the document.

3. Searching for Specific Publications:

If you're looking for a specific publication, you can use the search function located at the top of the page. Enter keywords related to the publication you're looking for, such as the title or a relevant topic.

The Pharmaceutical Guidance Navigator

Part 4 - Staying Informed: Resources for Ongoing Updates

Chapter 19: Regulatory Affairs Professionals Society (RAPS) for Regulatory News Updates

The Regulatory Affairs Professionals Society (RAPS) is a valuable resource for professionals in the pharmaceutical industry. RAPS offers a variety of educational and professional development opportunities, including certification programs, online courses, and industry resources. They also provide a platform for networking and career advancement. Overall, RAPS is a comprehensive resource that helps professionals stay up-to-date on the latest industry trends and regulations.

1. **Opening the Page:**

   - Open your web browser. Type in the URL: https://www.raps.org/news-and-articles/news-articles?page=1 or simply click on the link or scan QR code.

The Pharmaceutical Guidance Navigator

- You can see the following page.

2. Understanding the Page Layout:

- The page you land on is the first page of the News Articles section. It contains a list of news articles related to the Regulatory Affairs Professionals Society (RAPS).

- Each news article is represented by a card with a title, date, and brief description.

- The news articles are arranged in chronological order, with the most recent news at the top.

3. Navigating the List:

- You can scroll through the list to view the news articles.

- To read a news article, click on the title of the news article. This will take you to a page with the full text of the news article.

4. Reading a News Article:

- To read a news article, click on the title of the news article. This will take you to a page with the full text of the news article, along with any associated images or documents.

5. Searching for Specific News Articles:

If you're looking for a specific news article, you can use the search function located at the top of the page. Enter keywords related to the news article you're looking for, such as the title or a relevant topic.

The Pharmaceutical Guidance Navigator

Part 5 - Free Gift

As a token of my thanks for taking out time to read my book, I would like to offer you a **Free-Gift**:

Download your Free eBook PDF.

Directory of Global Health Authority Websites

List of 186 Website Links: A Comprehensive Directory of Global Health Authority Websites

To grab your **FREE GIFT** using the below URL or scanning the QR Code

https://pharmacydictionary.in/f7eei300k-4u-2/

The Pharmaceutical Guidance Navigator

About the Author

Karim Panjwani, a pharmacist, quality assurance professional, and technical writer, brings over 17 years of experience in the pharmaceutical industry. He has collaborated with leading multinational companies to establish quality systems that adhere to various regulatory bodies, including the U.S. FDA, MHRA, EU GMP, Health Canada, TGA, ANVISA, and WHO Geneva.

His area of expertise encompasses oral solid dosage, sterile, and nasal formulations. He possesses a profound understanding of the manufacturing and utility equipment used in pharmaceutical formulation production. Karim is adept at drafting and editing technical documents such as procedures, processes, investigations, risk assessments, and regulatory communications. He has a comprehensive understanding and practical knowledge of global regulations concerning the manufacture, storage, and distribution of pharmaceutical medicines.

Karim is passionate about disseminating his knowledge and insights through his papers and blogs. These cover a range of topics, including good documentation practice, regulatory expectations, quality culture, and cleaning validation.

Karim has hosted online pharmacy dictionary, https://pharmacydictionary.in/ with more than

12000 pharmaceutical terminologies and its meaning in simple language that is easy to understand. Karim has also developed an AI based online pharmacy dictionary, https://pharmacydictionary.in/ai-pharmacy-dictionary/ which also provides the meaning words in Hindi, Gujarati, Arabic, French, German and Russian language.

www.ingramcontent.com/pod-product-compliance
Lightning Source LLC
Chambersburg PA
CBHW050057230526
45470CB00004B/1567